Halloween Adventure in the Haunted House

Millan Trey

Published by Perfect Readers, 2024.

While every precaution has been taken in the preparation of this book, the publisher assumes no responsibility for errors or omissions, or for damages resulting from the use of the information contained herein.

HALLOWEEN ADVENTURE IN THE HAUNTED HOUSE

First edition. October 25, 2024.

ISBN: 979-8227498762

Written by Millan Trey.

Table of Contents

Description

On Halloween night, Joe, Ann, Mandy, and Matt set out to explore Grimwood Mansion, the eerie old house on the edge of town, known for its ghostly legends.

Inside, they face dark secrets and a sinister spirit known as the Shadow Man, who traps souls with endless greed. Joined by Sophie, a mysterious girl with her own connection to the house, the friends must summon courage, unravel the mansion's haunting history, and fight to escape.

With each chilling encounter, their bond grows, leading them to discover the strength found in friendship and bravery against all odds.

Dedication

To every young adventurer who dares to imagine, explore, and believe in the magic of friendship. May this story remind you of the strength found in unity and the courage to face the unknown together. And to those who cherish a good ghost story—this one's for you.

Preface

Halloween is a night of wonder, fear, and mystery.

In every town, tales of haunted houses and restless spirits come to life, woven with truths and myths that spark our imaginations. Grimwood Mansion, a dark relic of a forgotten past, has long cast shadows over the small town, leaving residents intrigued yet wary. In this story, you'll meet Joe, Ann, Mandy, Matt, and Sophie, who together find themselves drawn into the mansion's hidden depths. Facing terrors beyond imagination, they learn the true power of friendship.

May their adventure inspire your own journey into the unknown, where courage can light the way.

Chapter 1: The Dare

It was a chilly Halloween afternoon, and the sun was beginning to dip behind the orange and red trees of Maplewood Park. The leaves crunched underfoot as Joe, Ann, Mandy, and Matt sat at their usual hangout spot—the old wooden bench near the playground. Dressed in their casual clothes, the group was still contemplating what kind of fun they'd get up to that evening. After all, Halloween only came once a year, and for kids their age, it was always about finding the most thrilling adventure.

Joe, the oldest of the group at thirteen, leaned back on the bench, his brown hair slightly tousled by the wind. He was known for being brave, even a little too brave sometimes, and today was no exception. "You guys know what we should do tonight, right?" he said, a mischievous grin spreading across his face.

Ann, Joe's younger sister by a year, rolled her eyes. She was used to Joe's wild ideas, and most of the time, they ended up in trouble. "Let me guess. It involves doing something completely insane?"

Mandy, always the voice of reason, raised an eyebrow. "Joe, if you're planning on suggesting something dangerous, count me out."

Matt, Joe's best friend since kindergarten, leaned in, eyes wide with anticipation. "Come on, Mandy, where's your sense of adventure? I'm in, Joe. What's the plan?"

Joe paused for dramatic effect, looking at each of them before pointing toward the distant outline of a dark, looming structure at the edge of town—the old Grimwood Mansion.

"We spend the night there," he said, his voice low and full of excitement.

Mandy's jaw dropped, and Ann's eyes widened. "The haunted house?" Ann asked, incredulous. "You can't be serious. No one goes there, not even on Halloween."

"That's because everyone's too scared," Joe replied, his grin widening. "But think about it. The place has been abandoned for decades. There's probably nothing in there except dust and cobwebs. It's just an old house."

Mandy crossed her arms, her black curls bouncing as she shook her head. "There are a lot of stories about that place, Joe. And they aren't the 'just an old house' kind. People say it's haunted. And what about that boy who went missing last Halloween?"

"That's just a rumor," Joe argued. "Besides, we'll be together. Nothing can happen if we stick together, right, Matt?"

Matt, always ready for a challenge, nodded enthusiastically. "Right! It's Halloween! What better way to spend the night than in a haunted house? I bet we'll find something cool in there."

Ann, who had been quiet until now, spoke up. "You know Mom and Dad would ground us for life if they found out we went there, right?"

Joe waved her concern away. "We'll be home before anyone even notices we're gone. We just need to go in, check it out, and leave. Easy."

Mandy still wasn't convinced. "And what if something happens? What if the stories are true?"

Joe's eyes sparkled with determination. "Then we'll have the best Halloween story ever."

Ann looked at her brother and sighed. She knew there was no talking him out of it once his mind was set. And truth be told, a part of her was curious. The old Grimwood Mansion had always been a subject of mystery and fascination in their small town. People said it was cursed, haunted by the spirits of those who had died within its walls. It was the kind of place you dared your friends to go near, but no one ever did.

After a moment, Ann nodded. "Fine. I'm in."

Mandy glanced around at her friends. Joe was grinning, Matt was bouncing with excitement, and even Ann seemed intrigued. Despite her better judgment, she didn't want to be the only one left out. With a deep breath, she relented. "Alright. I'll come too. But if we get caught, I'm telling my parents it was all your idea, Joe."

Joe laughed. "Deal."

With the plan set, the group spent the rest of the afternoon preparing. They stopped by their homes to grab flashlights, extra batteries, and warm clothes. As night began to fall, they regrouped at the park, the excitement in the air building with every passing minute.

The streets of Maplewood were filled with children in costumes, trick-or-treating and laughing as they went door to door. The occasional sound of laughter and chatter echoed through the crisp air, but the group's thoughts were solely on the haunted mansion ahead.

The Grimwood Mansion stood at the edge of town, past the old cemetery and just beyond the last row of houses. It had been abandoned for as long as anyone could remember. Its towering, weather-beaten structure was cloaked in shadows, the windows dark and empty, like soulless eyes watching the town from afar.

As the group approached the mansion, a feeling of unease settled over them. The tall iron gates that surrounded the property were rusted and slightly ajar, as if inviting them in.

"Okay, we're really doing this," Matt said, his voice filled with both excitement and nerves.

Ann shone her flashlight at the gate, the beam cutting through the darkness. "It doesn't look as bad as I thought it would," she said, though her voice lacked conviction.

Mandy bit her lip. "I can't believe I let you talk me into this."

Joe pushed the gate open with a loud creak, the sound echoing through the empty street. "There's no turning back now," he said, stepping through the gate. "Come on."

One by one, the others followed him, their footsteps crunching on the gravel path that led to the front door. The mansion loomed above them, its towering structure casting long, eerie shadows under the dim moonlight.

When they reached the front steps, Joe reached for the old brass doorknob. The door groaned as he pushed it open, revealing a dark, cavernous entryway. Dust motes floated in the air, illuminated by their flashlights.

"Welcome to Grimwood Mansion," Joe said with a grin, though his voice was tinged with a hint of nervousness.

As they stepped inside, the door creaked shut behind them with an ominous thud.

For a moment, they all stood there in the dark silence, the weight of the mansion's eerie atmosphere pressing in around them. It was cold, much colder than outside, and the stillness was unsettling.

Ann was the first to break the silence. "Okay, so what now?"

Joe glanced around, his flashlight casting long shadows on the walls. "Now, we explore."

As they ventured deeper into the mansion, a strange feeling began to settle over them. It was as if the house itself was watching, waiting. What had started as a fun dare was quickly becoming something far more sinister.

And none of them could shake the feeling that they weren't alone.

Chapter 2: Meeting Mr. Grimwood

The inside of the Grimwood Mansion was as eerie as the outside, if not more so. The grand foyer stretched high above their heads, with cobweb-covered chandeliers and walls lined with portraits of people whose eyes seemed to follow their every move. A thick layer of dust coated the old wooden floors, and every step they took made the floorboards creak loudly, breaking the silence.

Joe led the way, his flashlight cutting through the gloom. "It's not that bad," he said, his voice trying to sound casual but betraying a hint of unease. "Just old and dusty."

Ann wasn't convinced. "I don't know, Joe. Something feels... off."

Mandy nodded in agreement, keeping her flashlight trained on the corners of the room as if expecting something to jump out. "I can feel it too. Like we're being watched."

Matt, trying to lighten the mood, chuckled nervously. "Maybe it's just the old portraits. They've got those creepy eyes that follow you around."

He shone his light on one particularly large portrait of a stern-looking man in a top hat. The man's gaze was cold, his eyes dark and piercing even through the layers of dust. Matt quickly shifted his light away.

"Let's keep moving," Joe suggested, trying to keep the group focused. "We'll explore a few rooms and then head out. In and out, no big deal."

The group cautiously moved deeper into the mansion, passing under archways and through long hallways filled with strange, old furniture and decor. The air inside the house felt heavy, as though it hadn't been disturbed in decades. Every now and then, they would hear the distant sound of something creaking, but when they stopped to listen, the noise would disappear.

After several minutes of exploring, they found themselves in what appeared to be a sitting room. The furniture was draped in white sheets, and the fireplace at the far end was dark and cold. The large, floor-length windows were covered in heavy curtains, blocking out what little moonlight might have made its way inside.

"This place is a lot bigger than I thought," Mandy whispered, keeping close to the others.

Joe nodded, shining his flashlight around the room. "Yeah, it's like a maze in here."

As they crossed the room, the sound of footsteps suddenly echoed from somewhere behind them. They all froze, their breath catching in their throats. For a moment, no one moved. The footsteps continued, slow and deliberate, as if someone—or something—was following them.

Ann gripped Joe's arm. "What was that?" she whispered, her voice trembling.

Joe tightened his grip on the flashlight. "I don't know."

Before anyone could say anything else, the footsteps stopped. Silence fell over the room, and the group exchanged nervous glances.

Suddenly, from the shadows in the corner of the room, an old, raspy voice broke the silence. "You shouldn't be here."

The group jumped, their flashlights immediately snapping to the source of the voice. There, standing in the corner, was an old man. His figure was hunched, and his face was partially hidden by a wide-brimmed hat. He wore a long, tattered coat that looked like it hadn't been washed in years. His eyes, though aged, were sharp and gleamed with an unsettling knowledge.

"Who—who are you?" Joe stammered, stepping in front of the group protectively.

The old man stepped forward into the light, his weathered face now visible. He had a grizzled beard, and his eyes were dark and sunken. He carried a gnarled wooden cane, though he didn't seem to need it for support.

"Name's Grimwood," the old man said slowly, his voice thick with age. "This was my family's house, once."

Mandy's eyes widened. "Wait... Grimwood? As in the mansion's name?"

The old man nodded, his gaze never leaving them. "Aye. My family lived here many years ago. But this house hasn't been a home for a long time. Not since... the curse."

Ann, always the curious one, stepped closer, despite the uneasy feeling gnawing at her stomach. "What curse? What happened here?"

Mr. Grimwood's expression darkened, and he let out a deep, tired sigh. "The house... it's alive, you see. Not in the way a person or animal is alive, but in a darker, more twisted way. It feeds on fear, on the souls of those who dare to enter. My ancestors... they dabbled in things they shouldn't have. Dark magic, forbidden rituals. They awoke something in this place, something that still lingers."

Matt, ever the skeptic, tried to play it off. "Come on, this sounds like one of those urban legends. There's no such thing as a haunted house."

Mr. Grimwood's eyes flashed with an intensity that made Matt take a step back. "Do you think I'm telling you stories, boy?" he growled. "I've seen things in this house that would make your blood run cold. Children like you... they come here, thinking it's all fun and games. But they never leave. This house doesn't let them."

Ann's heart skipped a beat. "What do you mean, 'never leave'?"

The old man's voice lowered, becoming almost a whisper. "There are others trapped in this house. Spirits. Lost souls. And there's something else—a shadow, a darkness that watches, waiting for those foolish enough to stay too long. The house will change around you. Doors will disappear. Rooms will shift. Time will slip away before you even realize it."

Joe, though unnerved, tried to keep his composure. "Why are you here, then? If the house is so dangerous, why haven't you left?"

Mr. Grimwood gave a bitter smile. "I'm part of this place now. It won't let me go. I've tried, but each time I step out those doors, I find myself right back inside. The house has its ways."

Mandy's voice trembled as she spoke. "If we're trapped... how do we get out?"

For the first time, Mr. Grimwood's expression softened, as though he pitied them. "There's only one way to escape. You must face the darkness that haunts this house. You have to outsmart it. But it's no easy task. Many have tried, and none have succeeded."

Joe exchanged glances with his friends. The idea of leaving now seemed more appealing than ever, but something about the old man's words made him pause. "So you're saying there's a way out?"

Mr. Grimwood nodded. "Perhaps. But the house will try to stop you at every turn. It'll use your fears against you. It'll make you question what's real and what's not. You'll have to be strong. Together."

Ann, her voice steady despite her fear, spoke up. "We can do it. We've been through tough stuff before."

Mandy wasn't so sure. "But this is different, Ann. This isn't just some game."

Joe turned to Mr. Grimwood, determination filling his voice. "We're not going to stay here. We'll find a way out."

The old man sighed. "Then be on your guard. The house knows you're here now. It'll start playing its games soon."

With that, Mr. Grimwood turned and disappeared into the shadows, leaving the group standing in stunned silence.

Chapter 3: The Haunted House

The silence after Mr. Grimwood's departure was suffocating. His warning lingered in the air like a thick fog, making every creak of the floorboards and whisper of the wind feel like something more sinister. The group stood huddled together in the sitting room, their flashlights casting long, eerie shadows on the walls. Each of them felt it—the sense that the mansion had somehow changed after Mr. Grimwood's appearance.

"Do you think he was telling the truth?" Ann asked quietly, her voice barely above a whisper.

Joe didn't answer immediately. He didn't want to admit it, but something about Mr. Grimwood's story had unsettled him. He wasn't sure if it was the way the old man had spoken, his cryptic warnings, or the fact that Grimwood Mansion already felt alive with strange energy, but Joe couldn't shake the feeling that they were in way over their heads.

"I don't know," Joe finally said, his voice uncertain. "But we can't just stand around waiting for something to happen. We need to move. Let's stick together and find a way out."

Ann, ever the rational one, nodded. "Right. The sooner we get out of here, the better."

Mandy glanced around nervously. "I still don't like this. The house... it feels different now. Like it's watching us."

Matt, trying to keep his usual bravado, added, "It's just an old house. We'll be fine. We've got flashlights, we've got each other. What's the worst that could happen?"

The group moved as one, walking back into the grand foyer. The dim light from their flashlights revealed the same towering ceilings and dusty furniture, but now there was something different. It was as if the air had grown colder, heavier. The portraits on the walls, once silent observers, now seemed more alive, their painted eyes following every movement the group made.

Joe pointed his flashlight toward the grand staircase that led to the second floor. "We haven't been upstairs yet. There might be another way out up there."

Ann hesitated. "Do you really think it's a good idea to go deeper into the house?"

"We've already come this far," Joe replied. "We might as well explore all our options."

With some reluctance, the group made their way to the base of the staircase. The steps creaked loudly under their weight, as if protesting their intrusion. The bannister was cold and slick with dust, and the air grew even chillier as they ascended.

As they reached the top, the second floor stretched out before them in a maze of hallways and closed doors. The wallpaper was peeling in places, and cobwebs draped the corners like ghostly decorations. The eerie silence was occasionally broken by the soft creak of the floor beneath them or the distant sound of something shifting in the house.

"This place is huge," Matt whispered, shining his light down one of the long corridors. "How are we supposed to find anything in here?"

"We start by sticking together," Joe said firmly. "We'll check each room until we find something—anything—that might help us figure out what's going on."

The group moved cautiously, opening one door after another. Each room they entered seemed more bizarre than the last. There was a bedroom with a four-poster bed draped in decaying curtains, an old study filled with crumbling books and papers, and a drawing room where the furniture looked like it hadn't been touched in centuries. But there was something else, too—a feeling of being watched, of something lurking just beyond the edge of their flashlights.

It wasn't long before Mandy, always the most sensitive to the atmosphere around her, stopped in the middle of the hallway. "Do you guys hear that?"

The others froze, straining their ears. For a moment, there was nothing but the sound of their own breathing. Then, faintly, they heard it—a soft whispering sound, like the wind moving through the walls.

"It's probably just the house settling," Joe said, trying to keep everyone calm, though he didn't quite believe his own words.

But the whispering grew louder, more distinct. The voices seemed to echo from every direction, and they weren't random sounds anymore—they were words.

"I can't... make it out," Ann said, her face pale. "It sounds like... like they're saying our names."

Matt tried to laugh it off. "Okay, now this is getting creepy."

Suddenly, the door to the room at the end of the hallway creaked open on its own. The group's flashlights snapped to it immediately, their beams illuminating the dark, gaping entrance.

"I guess we're going in there next," Joe muttered, his voice tense.

They approached the open door cautiously, peering inside. It was another sitting room, much like the one downstairs, but this one had an air of abandonment that was even more pronounced. Dust covered everything in thick layers, and the fireplace at the far end was cracked and broken.

But what caught their attention was the mirror.

A large, ornate mirror hung on the wall opposite the door, its surface grimy and smudged with age. As they stepped inside, the group's flashlights reflected off the glass, casting strange patterns across the room.

Ann was the first to notice something odd. "Look at the mirror."

The others turned their lights on the mirror, and their blood ran cold. Instead of their reflections, the mirror showed something else—other faces, ghostly and pale, staring back at them. Children, their eyes wide with fear, their hands pressed against the glass as if trying to escape.

"What the...?" Matt whispered, stepping back in shock.

Mandy clutched Joe's arm, her voice shaking. "Joe, what's happening?"

"I don't know," Joe replied, his voice tight with fear. "But we need to get out of here. Now."

Just as they turned to leave, the door slammed shut with a deafening bang. The group jumped, their flashlights shaking in their hands.

"We're trapped!" Ann cried, running to the door and pulling on the handle. It didn't budge.

The whispering grew louder, filling the room with an oppressive, suffocating energy. The children in the mirror began to move, their mouths forming silent words, their eyes pleading for help.

Joe's mind raced as he searched for a way out. "Look for another door, a window, anything!"

But there were no other doors, no windows that weren't nailed shut. The only exit was the door they had come through, and it was sealed tight.

Mandy, her breath coming in shallow gasps, pointed to the mirror. "It's... it's moving!"

The group turned back to the mirror just in time to see the faces of the children fading away, replaced by something darker—something far more terrifying. A shadowy figure began to take shape in the glass, its form tall and menacing, its eyes glowing with a sickly, unnatural light.

The figure seemed to step out of the mirror, its shadowy arms reaching toward them.

"Run!" Joe shouted, but there was nowhere to run. The door was locked, and the figure was closing in.

Ann screamed as the figure's cold, shadowy hand brushed against her arm, sending a wave of icy fear through her body.

Joe grabbed her and pulled her back, his heart pounding. "We have to break the mirror!"

Matt, without thinking, grabbed a heavy vase from the mantel and hurled it at the mirror. The glass shattered with an earsplitting crash, and the shadowy figure dissolved into smoke, disappearing into the air.

The door suddenly swung open, and the group stumbled out of the room, gasping for breath.

"We... we need to leave," Mandy said, her voice trembling. "We need to leave right now."

Joe nodded, his face pale. "Agreed. Let's get out of here."

But as they made their way back toward the staircase, they realized something horrifying. The hallway they had just come through was no longer there. The walls had shifted, closing off the way they had come. The house was changing around them, trapping them deeper inside.

Joe's voice was grim as he spoke. "We're not getting out that easily."

The mansion had other plans for them.

Chapter 4: The Door That Locked Itself

The mansion seemed to be alive. Every corner the group turned, every door they tried, felt like it was part of some twisted game the house was playing with them. The hallway they had just walked down was gone, and in its place, the walls stretched endlessly, leading them into a maze of confusion and fear.

"We're stuck," Mandy whispered, her voice trembling as she clutched her flashlight tightly. "The house is shifting around us. We'll never find our way out."

Joe, trying his best to stay calm, shook his head. "No, we will. We just need to stay focused. There has to be another way. There's always a way."

The others didn't look so sure. Ann's face was pale, and Matt had gone unusually quiet, the reality of their situation starting to weigh heavily on all of them. Even Joe, the one who had pushed for this adventure in the first place, was feeling the crushing weight of fear in his chest.

They pressed on, choosing a hallway at random, hoping it would lead them back toward the staircase or another exit. The floors creaked beneath their feet, and the walls seemed to close in around them as if the house itself were breathing. Every so often, a soft whisper would drift through the air, just loud enough to send chills down their spines but too quiet to understand.

After what felt like an eternity of walking through the seemingly endless hallways, they reached a door. It was a large, wooden door with intricate carvings along its edges, the kind that looked like it belonged to some grand ballroom or library.

Joe stepped forward cautiously, his hand reaching for the doorknob. "Let's see what's behind this one."

Ann grabbed his arm. "Wait, Joe. What if—"

Before she could finish, the door creaked open on its own.

The group froze, staring at the door in shock. It swung inward slowly, revealing a dark, cavernous room beyond. The air that flowed out was thick and musty, carrying with it the scent of something old and forgotten.

Matt swallowed hard. "I don't like this. I really don't like this."

But Joe had already stepped inside. His flashlight beam cut through the darkness, revealing the outlines of tall shelves, like the kind you'd find in a library, only these were covered in dust and cobwebs. Ancient books lined the shelves, their spines cracked and their pages yellowed with age.

"This must be some kind of study," Joe muttered, stepping further into the room. "Maybe there's something here that can help us figure out how to get out."

The others hesitated at the doorway but eventually followed him in. The room felt colder than the rest of the house, as if the air itself had frozen in time. The only sound was the soft crunch of their footsteps on the dusty floor.

Ann approached one of the shelves, her flashlight illuminating the titles of the books. Most of them were written in languages she didn't recognize, but one caught her eye—*The History of Grimwood Manor.* She pulled it from the shelf, coughing as a cloud of dust billowed up around her.

"Guys, look at this," she said, showing the book to the others.

Joe leaned in, curious. "Maybe this will tell us more about the house."

As Ann opened the book, the pages crackled with age. She flipped through them quickly, scanning for anything that might explain what was happening to them. But most of the text was unreadable, faded and smeared. What she could make out was cryptic and unsettling, mentioning curses, dark rituals, and a man known only as *The Shadow Man.*

Mandy, standing near the door, shivered. "I really don't like this place. Can we just—"

The door slammed shut with a deafening bang.

Everyone jumped, their flashlights flickering wildly as they turned toward the door. Matt rushed over, pulling on the handle, but it wouldn't budge. "It's locked! I can't get it open!"

Panic set in as they realized they were trapped. The room suddenly felt smaller, the walls seeming to close in on them.

"Let me try," Joe said, pushing past Matt to tug on the door. But no matter how hard he pulled, the door wouldn't open. It was as if it had sealed itself shut, trapping them inside.

Ann's heart raced as she backed away from the door. "This is just like what Mr. Grimwood said. The house is trapping us."

Mandy, her voice rising in fear, asked, "What are we going to do? We can't stay in here forever!"

Joe, his jaw clenched in frustration, looked around the room, searching for another way out. His flashlight swept over the shelves, the desk, the fireplace at the far end. Nothing seemed out of the ordinary—just an old, forgotten study.

But then, as his light passed over the far wall, something strange happened. The wall began to shimmer, as though it were made of liquid instead of solid wood. For a brief moment, it rippled like water, and then the shimmering stopped.

"Did you guys see that?" Joe whispered, his eyes wide.

The others turned their flashlights toward the wall, but it looked normal again—just a plain wooden wall, covered in dust and cobwebs.

"What was it?" Matt asked, taking a step closer.

"I don't know," Joe admitted, "but I think it's something important. Maybe it's another way out."

Ann frowned. "A wall? How could that be—"

Before she could finish, the wall began to ripple again. This time, the effect lasted longer, and as the wall shimmered, an outline of a door began to form.

Mandy gasped. "It's a door! But how?"

Joe didn't wait to find out. He hurried over to the wall, reaching out to touch the shimmering outline. His hand passed through it, as if the wall weren't there at all. "It's not solid," he said, his voice filled with awe and confusion. "It's like... an illusion."

Ann, cautiously optimistic, stepped closer. "Do you think it's safe?"

Joe glanced back at her. "Do we have any other choice?"

The group exchanged nervous glances, but it was clear they all felt the same. They had to get out of the room, and this was their only option. Joe took a deep breath and stepped through the shimmering doorway.

For a moment, the world seemed to tilt around him. There was a sensation of cold air rushing past, a flash of darkness, and then he was standing in another hallway, this one dimly lit by a series of old, flickering sconces on the walls.

Ann, Matt, and Mandy followed, stepping through the illusion one by one. As soon as they were all on the other side, the shimmering door vanished, leaving them once again at the mercy of the mansion's maze-like structure.

"We made it out," Ann said, her voice a mixture of relief and disbelief. "But where are we now?"

Joe looked around, his flashlight revealing more of the strange hallway. The walls here were covered in peeling wallpaper, and the air smelled faintly of damp earth. It was unlike any other part of the mansion they had seen so far.

"I don't know," Joe replied, "but we need to keep moving."

They began to walk down the hallway, the floorboards creaking beneath their feet with every step. The sconces flickered ominously as they passed, casting eerie shadows on the walls.

As they walked, Ann flipped through the book she had taken from the study, her brow furrowed in concentration. "This book mentions something about a man called the Shadow Man," she said quietly. "I think he's connected to whatever is happening in this house."

Joe's stomach churned at the mention of the name. "The Shadow Man? What does it say about him?"

Ann read aloud, her voice low and tense. "It says he's a spirit that haunts the mansion, feeding off the fear of those who enter. He can control the house, make it shift and change to trap his victims. It says the only way to escape is to confront him."

Matt's face went pale. "Confront him? Are you kidding? How are we supposed to do that?"

Joe's grip tightened on his flashlight. "We don't have a choice. If we want to get out of here, we're going to have to face whatever's controlling this place."

The group fell into a heavy silence as they continued down the hallway, each of them grappling with the growing sense of dread that hung over them. They had come to Grimwood Mansion for an adventure, but now it was clear that this was no ordinary haunted house.

Chapter 5: The Whispering Walls

The hallway stretched before them, dimly lit by the flickering sconces that lined the walls. Their footsteps echoed eerily in the silence, each creak of the floorboards a reminder that they were very much alone in the haunted mansion. Or at least, that's how it seemed.

Ann was still flipping through *The History of Grimwood Manor*, her brow furrowed as she tried to piece together more clues. Every so often, she would mutter something under her breath about *The Shadow Man*, but none of them really knew what they were up against yet.

Joe led the way, his flashlight scanning the walls for anything that looked like it might lead them out. The mansion was vast and maze-like, and after what felt like hours of wandering, they still hadn't found any exit. The feeling of being trapped was beginning to weigh heavily on them.

But it wasn't just the layout of the mansion that was unnerving. As they walked, the whispering began again.

At first, it was faint, almost like the wind moving through cracks in the old house. But then it grew louder, more distinct. It wasn't just random noise anymore. It was voices.

Ann slowed down, her eyes widening. "Do you hear that?"

The others stopped, their flashlights wavering as they listened. The whispering seemed to come from the walls themselves, surrounding them on all sides. It was a low, insistent murmur, but if they focused hard enough, they could make out words.

"I don't like this," Mandy whispered, her arms hugging her body tightly as if to protect herself from the chill in the air.

Matt's flashlight beam flickered, casting jittery shadows along the walls. "It's probably just the wind," he said, though the uncertainty in his voice was clear.

But Ann shook her head, her face pale. "No, it's not the wind. It's... it's saying our names."

For a moment, no one moved. The whispers, still faint, seemed to grow louder as if responding to Ann's words. Joe strained to listen, and sure enough, he could hear it: his name. Faint, almost inaudible, but definitely there. It was as though the walls themselves were alive, calling out to them in ghostly voices.

"Joe... Ann... Mandy... Matt..."

Joe's stomach twisted with fear. "We need to keep moving. Don't stop."

But the whispers followed them. As they moved deeper into the hallway, the voices grew louder, more urgent. They were no longer just saying names—they were speaking in full sentences now, though it was hard to make out what they were saying. It was like listening to a conversation underwater, distorted and strange.

Suddenly, Ann stopped in her tracks. Her flashlight beam was fixed on a section of the wall where the wallpaper had peeled away, revealing the wooden boards underneath. "Look at this," she said, her voice shaky.

The others gathered around her, their flashlights illuminating the wall. Beneath the peeling wallpaper, something was carved into the wood. It was faint, but they could make out the words scratched into the surface as if someone had done it in a desperate hurry:

"We're still here."

Matt took a step back, his face pale. "What does that mean? Who's still here?"

Joe swallowed hard, the dread in his chest growing heavier by the second. "The people Mr. Grimwood talked about. The ones who got trapped here."

Mandy looked like she was about to cry. "We need to get out of here. This isn't just some haunted house—there are real spirits here."

The whispering seemed to swell in response to her words, growing louder and more aggressive. The voices were coming from every direction now, overlapping in a cacophony of sounds that made it impossible to tell where they were coming from.

Ann clutched the book tightly, her knuckles white. "There's something about this in the book. The house... it feeds on fear. The more scared we get, the stronger it becomes."

Joe tried to keep his voice steady, but it was becoming harder to stay calm. "Then we need to stay calm. Let's keep moving."

They continued down the hallway, but the whispering only intensified. It was as though the house was alive, taunting them, trying to drive them deeper into panic. The walls themselves seemed to shift and pulse with every step they took, as if the house was breathing in time with their fear.

Just as they thought they couldn't take it anymore, they reached another door. It was an old, wooden door, similar to the others they had passed, but something about this one felt different. It was as though the door was calling to them, urging them to open it.

Joe hesitated, his hand hovering over the doorknob. "Should we?"

"We have to," Ann said. "There might be something in there that can help us."

Taking a deep breath, Joe turned the knob. The door creaked open, revealing a small, dimly lit room. Unlike the rest of the mansion, which felt cold and abandoned, this room had a strange warmth to it. The walls were lined with old portraits, and a single chair sat in the center of the room, facing a large mirror.

Mandy stepped inside cautiously, her flashlight sweeping the room. "What is this place?"

Joe approached the mirror, his reflection staring back at him. It seemed ordinary enough, but there was something unsettling about it, as if the reflection wasn't quite... right. He felt a strange pull toward the glass, like it was drawing him in.

Suddenly, Ann gasped. "Look!"

She pointed to the portraits on the walls. At first, they looked like ordinary old paintings, their subjects dressed in the fashion of the mansion's heyday. But as they looked closer, they realized that the faces in the portraits were changing.

The painted eyes were moving.

One by one, the portraits' eyes shifted, following the group's every movement. The faces, once serene and composed, began to twist into expressions of fear and desperation. It was as though the people in the paintings were trying to communicate with them, trapped in the frames just as they were trapped in the mansion.

Mandy let out a soft whimper. "This place is cursed."

Ann's voice was barely a whisper. "They're the ones who never made it out. The ones the house took."

Joe tore his gaze away from the mirror, his heart pounding in his chest. "We need to go. Now."

But as he turned toward the door, something strange happened. The whispering, which had been relentless since they entered the hallway, suddenly stopped. The silence was deafening, and the air in the room felt thick and heavy.

Then, without warning, the door slammed shut.

Matt rushed to the door, pulling on the handle, but it wouldn't budge. "It's locked again! We're trapped!"

The group's flashlights flickered, casting strange, dancing shadows on the walls. The portraits seemed to leer down at them, their faces twisted in terror. And then, from the mirror, a low, guttural voice echoed through the room.

"Leave... now..."

Joe spun around, his flashlight fixed on the mirror. The surface of the glass had changed—it was no longer reflecting the room. Instead, it showed a dark, swirling vortex, as if the mirror itself had become a portal to some other place. And in the center of the swirling darkness, a figure began to take shape.

It was tall, its form shrouded in shadow, with glowing red eyes that seemed to pierce through the darkness.

"The Shadow Man," Ann whispered, her voice trembling with fear.

Joe's pulse raced as he backed away from the mirror, his eyes locked on the figure inside. The Shadow Man reached out, his long, bony fingers stretching toward the glass, as if he were trying to break through.

"We have to get out of here!" Joe shouted, pulling on the door with all his strength. But it wouldn't open. It was as though the house was determined to keep them trapped.

The Shadow Man's voice echoed again, this time louder, more insistent. "You will never leave..."

Mandy screamed as the figure in the mirror lunged forward, its hand pressing against the glass. The surface rippled, and for a moment, it looked like the Shadow Man was going to break through.

But just as the glass seemed to give way, Ann grabbed the book and slammed it against the mirror. The impact sent a sharp crack through the glass, and the figure inside recoiled with a deafening screech.

The whispering stopped. The portraits went still. The room fell into an eerie silence once again.

Joe wasted no time. With one final pull, the door gave way, and they stumbled out into the hallway, their hearts racing and their breath coming in short gasps.

Chapter 6: Sophie Appears

The hallway stretched before them, unfamiliar and seemingly endless. The mansion had shifted again, and the door they had just escaped through had vanished into the walls behind them. Every corner they turned seemed to lead them deeper into the twisted maze of Grimwood Mansion, and each step felt heavier with the growing realization that the house wasn't just haunted—it was alive.

"We've got to get out of here," Joe said, his voice barely masking the panic rising inside him. His flashlight flickered as he scanned the new hallway. The walls were lined with the same peeling wallpaper, and the floorboards creaked beneath their feet, but there was something different about this part of the house. The air felt colder, thicker, as if they were descending deeper into the mansion's heart.

Ann nodded, clutching *The History of Grimwood Manor* to her chest as if it might somehow protect them. "I don't think we're alone anymore," she whispered. "That thing in the mirror—The Shadow Man—it's watching us."

Matt, usually the one to crack jokes in tense situations, was uncharacteristically silent, his face pale and his hands trembling as he followed behind the others. "I don't want to see that thing again," he muttered. "We need to find a way out before it shows up."

Mandy trailed behind, casting nervous glances over her shoulder. The portraits, the whispers, the shifting walls—it all felt like too much. She had always been the cautious one, but now her fear was palpable. "What if there isn't a way out?" she asked, her voice barely above a whisper. "What if we're stuck here... like the others?"

Joe didn't want to answer that question. The thought of being trapped in the mansion forever, haunted by The Shadow Man, sent chills down his spine. He needed to focus, to find a way to keep the group moving, but every door they opened seemed to lead to another dead end, another dark hallway. It was as if the mansion was toying with them, slowly tightening its grip.

Just as Joe was about to suggest they turn back, they heard it—footsteps. Faint at first, but unmistakable. Someone else was walking through the house.

Ann froze, her flashlight trembling in her hand. "Did you hear that?"

Joe nodded, signaling for the others to be quiet. The footsteps were coming closer, echoing through the empty halls. Whoever—or whatever—was approaching wasn't trying to hide.

They huddled together, waiting, their breath held as the sound of the footsteps grew louder. Joe tightened his grip on his flashlight, ready to swing it if necessary. His heart raced as a figure emerged from the shadows at the far end of the hallway.

It was a girl, no older than them, with long dark hair and a pale complexion. She wore a simple, old-fashioned dress, and her eyes were wide with a mix of curiosity and fear. She looked almost out of place, as if she had wandered out of another time.

"Who... who are you?" Joe asked, taking a cautious step forward.

The girl stopped in her tracks, her eyes darting between them as if she wasn't sure whether to trust them. "My name's Sophie," she said, her voice soft but clear. "I've been stuck in this house for a long time."

Ann's eyes widened. "You've been here? For how long?"

Sophie looked down at her feet, her expression troubled. "I don't know anymore. Days, weeks... maybe even years. The house makes you lose track of time."

Matt stepped forward, his fear momentarily replaced by disbelief. "How is that even possible? You mean you've just been wandering around this place all this time?"

Sophie nodded. "It's not easy to escape. The house... it changes. It traps people, keeps them here. I've seen others come and go, but most of them never make it out."

Joe's heart sank. Sophie's words confirmed what they had all been dreading. The house was more than just a haunted mansion—it was a prison. "How do we get out?" he asked, his voice filled with urgency. "There has to be a way."

Sophie hesitated, glancing around nervously as if she feared the house might be listening. "There's a way," she said quietly. "But it's dangerous. The house won't let you leave unless you break its hold. And to do that, you have to face The Shadow Man."

At the mention of The Shadow Man, Ann's face drained of color. "We saw him," she whispered. "In the mirror. He... he tried to come through."

Sophie's expression darkened. "He's the one who controls the house. He feeds off fear. The more scared you are, the stronger he becomes. If you want to leave, you have to confront him—and you have to be brave."

Mandy shook her head, her voice trembling. "Confront him? Are you serious? We can't even look at him without freaking out."

Sophie stepped closer, her eyes locking onto Mandy's. "I know it sounds impossible, but it's the only way. The Shadow Man preys on fear. If you can stand up to him, if you can face him without being afraid, he loses his power. That's how you escape."

Joe glanced at his friends, their faces a mixture of fear and uncertainty. It was one thing to wander through a haunted house, but to actually confront the malevolent force that controlled it? It seemed like a suicide mission. But Sophie's calm confidence gave him hope. She had been here longer than any of them, and if anyone knew how to survive the mansion, it was her.

"How do we find him?" Joe asked, his voice firm. "Where is The Shadow Man?"

Sophie hesitated, as if the answer frightened her. "He's in the heart of the house. The ballroom. That's where he waits."

Matt groaned, running a hand through his hair. "Of course it's in a creepy ballroom. Why wouldn't it be?"

Ann, ever the practical one, stepped forward. "If the ballroom is where we need to go, then we need to figure out how to get there. This house keeps changing. How do we know the way?"

Sophie bit her lip, thinking. "I've been through this house a hundred times. I've learned a few things. The house tries to confuse you, but there are certain paths it can't change. The staircases, for example. They always lead somewhere important. If we can find the right staircase, it should take us to the ballroom."

Joe nodded, feeling a renewed sense of purpose. "Then let's go. Lead the way, Sophie."

The group, with Sophie now at the front, made their way down the twisting hallways. The mansion was quieter now, as if it knew they were getting closer to the heart of the house. The whispering had stopped, but the oppressive feeling of being watched lingered, a constant reminder that The Shadow Man was always near.

As they turned another corner, they reached a grand staircase, its banister carved with intricate designs that had long since faded with age. Sophie paused at the base of the stairs, her eyes scanning the shadows at the top.

"This is it," she said, her voice barely above a whisper. "Once we go up, there's no turning back. The house will know what we're trying to do."

Ann gripped Joe's arm, her eyes filled with fear. "Are we really doing this?"

Joe took a deep breath, his heart pounding in his chest. "We have to. It's the only way out."

With that, they began to ascend the staircase, their footsteps echoing in the eerie silence. The air grew colder with each step, and the shadows seemed to grow darker, deeper. The mansion was changing again, shifting in anticipation of the confrontation to come.

Sophie led them with steady determination, but Joe could see the fear in her eyes. She had been through this before, and she knew what awaited them. But she was brave, and her bravery gave them strength.

They reached the top of the stairs, and found themselves standing before a set of double doors, their surface worn and cracked with age. Beyond those doors lay the ballroom—the heart of the mansion and the lair of The Shadow Man.

Chapter 7: The Vanishing Staircase

The double doors creaked as they swung open, revealing the dark, ominous entrance to the ballroom. The air felt colder now, charged with the eerie energy that radiated from the heart of Grimwood Mansion. Joe, Ann, Mandy, Matt, and their new companion, Sophie, stood at the threshold, their flashlights flickering against the ancient, dust-filled air.

"This is it," Sophie said quietly, her voice barely a whisper. "The ballroom is where The Shadow Man waits."

Joe swallowed hard, trying to steady his nerves. The oppressive atmosphere seemed to press down on them from all sides, as though the house itself was watching their every move. He turned to his friends, giving them a nod of encouragement, though he wasn't sure he believed his own confidence.

Ann held tightly to *The History of Grimwood Manor,* her knuckles white as she clutched the book to her chest. "Are we ready for this?" she asked, her voice trembling with fear.

Mandy, who had been the most anxious of them all, took a deep breath. "We don't have a choice, do we? If we want to get out of here, we have to face him."

Matt tried to offer a small, brave smile, though his hands were shaking. "We've made it this far. No backing out now."

Sophie, who had been trapped in the mansion longer than any of them, took a step forward. "Just remember—he feeds on fear. The more afraid we are, the stronger he becomes. We have to be brave, no matter what we see in there."

With one final look at each other, they crossed the threshold into the ballroom.

The room was enormous, much larger than any other space they had seen in the mansion. It was once grand, that much was clear, but now it was a shell of its former self. The floors were cracked and covered in dust, and the once-beautiful chandeliers that hung from the ceiling were now dark and broken. Long, tattered curtains hung limply from the tall windows, their faded fabric fluttering slightly in the cold, still air.

But the most unsettling feature of the room was the large, cracked mirror that dominated one wall. It was the same mirror they had seen before—the one where The Shadow Man had first appeared. The sight of it sent a wave of dread through the group.

"Stay together," Joe whispered, his eyes fixed on the mirror. "Don't let him separate us."

They moved cautiously through the ballroom, their footsteps echoing in the vast, empty space. The air was thick with tension, and every shadow seemed to move, to stretch and reach toward them. The mansion's energy was stronger here, more oppressive, as if they were walking straight into its heart.

Suddenly, a low, guttural sound echoed through the room. It was faint at first, but it grew louder, more distinct—a deep, rasping breath that seemed to come from all around them.

"He's here," Sophie whispered, her voice tight with fear. "The Shadow Man."

Joe felt his stomach tighten as he scanned the room, his flashlight beam bouncing across the cracked floor and the dusty walls. But there was no sign of The Shadow Man—only the empty ballroom and the broken mirror.

Then, without warning, the doors slammed shut behind them.

Matt jumped, his flashlight flickering wildly as he spun around. "We're trapped!"

Panic set in as they rushed toward the doors, but no matter how hard they pulled, the doors wouldn't budge. It was as if the mansion had sealed them inside, determined to keep them in the ballroom with The Shadow Man.

"We need to find another way out!" Ann cried, her voice filled with urgency.

But before they could move, the mirror began to shimmer.

A thick, dark mist seeped from the cracks in the glass, swirling and twisting in the air. The mist gathered in the center of the room, slowly forming the shape of a tall, shadowy figure. The Shadow Man.

He was more terrifying in person than they could have imagined. His form was barely human, a mass of darkness and swirling mist, his glowing red eyes fixed on the group with malevolent intent. His long, bony fingers stretched out toward them, and the room seemed to grow even colder as his presence filled the space.

Joe's heart raced as the others backed away in fear. The Shadow Man's voice echoed through the ballroom, low and menacing. "You will never leave."

Sophie, standing at the front of the group, faced The Shadow Man with determination, though her hands were shaking. "We're not afraid of you," she said, her voice trembling but firm. "We know what you are. You can't keep us here."

The Shadow Man's eyes glowed brighter, his voice like a hiss. "I feed on your fear. You will never escape me."

As he spoke, the walls of the ballroom began to shift, twisting and warping as if the house itself was reacting to his words. The floor beneath their feet cracked and groaned, and the chandeliers above swayed dangerously.

"We need to get out of here!" Mandy cried, her voice rising in panic.

But before they could move, the ground beneath them began to shake. The floorboards cracked and splintered, and the entire room seemed to lurch. Joe stumbled, grabbing onto Ann to steady himself. "Hold on!"

The ballroom shook violently, and suddenly, the grand staircase that had brought them here began to vanish. Piece by piece, the steps dissolved into nothingness, leaving only empty space where the staircase had once been.

"Our way out!" Matt shouted, pointing to the empty space. "It's gone!"

The Shadow Man's laughter echoed through the ballroom, a cold, cruel sound that sent chills down their spines. "There is no escape."

Joe's mind raced as he searched for another way out. The ballroom was large, but with the staircase gone, there was no clear exit. The walls were shifting, the floor was cracking, and The Shadow Man was growing stronger with each passing second.

Ann gripped *The History of Grimwood Manor* tightly. "There has to be something in the book! Something that can stop him!"

She frantically flipped through the pages, her hands shaking as she searched for any clue, any spell or incantation that could weaken The Shadow Man's hold on the house. But the words were faded, the pages worn and smudged. She couldn't make sense of it.

"We don't have time!" Mandy shouted, her voice filled with terror.

The mist surrounding The Shadow Man began to spread, creeping across the floor like a living thing. It reached for them, cold and suffocating, as if trying to pull them into the darkness.

Joe stepped forward, his hands trembling but his voice steady. "We're not afraid of you!" he shouted, trying to summon the courage Sophie had spoken about. "You can't keep us here!"

The Shadow Man's eyes flickered, his form shifting in the swirling mist. For a moment, it seemed as though Joe's words had weakened him, but then the darkness surged forward, engulfing the room.

Sophie grabbed Joe's arm, pulling him back. "It's not enough. He's too strong."

Matt, his eyes wide with fear, pointed toward the far end of the room. "Look! Another door!"

At the opposite end of the ballroom, barely visible through the swirling mist, was a small, wooden door. It was half-hidden behind a heavy curtain, but it was there—a possible way out.

"That's our only chance!" Joe shouted. "Run!"

The group sprinted across the ballroom, dodging the cracks in the floor and the swirling tendrils of mist. The Shadow Man's laughter echoed behind them, but they didn't stop. They couldn't.

As they reached the door, Sophie pulled it open, and they all tumbled through, slamming it shut behind them. The sound of The Shadow Man's laughter faded as the door clicked shut, leaving them in a narrow, dark hallway.

They were safe—for now.

Joe leaned against the wall, breathing heavily, his heart pounding in his chest. "That was too close."

Ann, still clutching the book, shook her head, with a pale face. "He's getting stronger. We need to figure out how to stop him—fast."

Sophie, her face tight with worry, glanced back at the door. "We don't have much time. He won't stop until he has all of us."

The group huddled together, the weight of the mansion's dark magic pressing down on them. They were closer to The Shadow Man than ever before, and now, they were running out of time.

Chapter 8: The Phantom Lights

The hallway they found themselves in after escaping The Shadow Man was long and narrow, the air heavy with the musty scent of age and decay. Their footsteps echoed as they cautiously made their way through the corridor, each of them on edge after their close encounter in the ballroom. The wooden door they had slammed shut behind them felt like a flimsy barrier between them and the dark forces lurking in the house, but it was all they had for now.

"Are we safe?" Matt asked, glancing nervously over his shoulder. His voice was shaky, and he kept shifting his flashlight from side to side, as if expecting The Shadow Man to burst through the door at any second.

"For now," Sophie replied, her voice calm but tense. "But we can't stay here. We need to keep moving before the house shifts again."

Joe nodded, taking a deep breath to steady his nerves. He knew Sophie was right. The mansion was constantly changing, and if they stayed in one place too long, they might find themselves trapped. The fear of what had just happened in the ballroom still weighed heavily on him, but they couldn't afford to lose focus now.

"Let's go," he said, taking the lead once more. "Stay close. We'll figure this out."

The hallway seemed to stretch endlessly before them, the flickering beams of their flashlights barely piercing the darkness. As they walked, the walls seemed to press closer, the ceiling lower. It was as though the house itself was suffocating them, closing in to remind them that escape was not an option.

Ann was flipping through *The History of Grimwood Manor* as they walked, trying to make sense of the faded pages. "There has to be something in here," she muttered. "Something we missed."

But the text was difficult to read, the words old and smudged. Every page told the story of the mansion's dark past, of how The

Shadow Man had come to haunt it, feeding on the fear of those who wandered inside. But there was no clear answer, no simple solution to stop him.

"We'll figure it out," Joe reassured her, though he wasn't entirely sure of that himself. "We just have to keep moving."

They continued down the hallway, the tension growing with each step. The silence of the mansion was oppressive, broken only by the sound of their own breathing and the occasional creak of the floorboards. It felt like they were the only ones left in the world, lost in a maze of shadows and forgotten secrets.

Suddenly, Mandy stopped in her tracks, her flashlight flickering. "Do you see that?" she whispered, pointing ahead.

The others halted, their flashlights snapping toward where Mandy was pointing. At first, there was nothing but darkness. But then, faintly, they saw it—small, glowing orbs of light floating in the air at the far end of the hallway.

"What is that?" Matt asked, his voice a mix of curiosity and fear.

The orbs of light moved slowly, lazily drifting through the air as if they were carried on an invisible breeze. They shimmered with an eerie glow, casting strange, elongated shadows on the walls as they moved. The lights were beautiful in a haunting sort of way, their soft glow illuminating the otherwise dark corridor in a way that felt almost peaceful. But there was something unsettling about them too—something that made the hair on the back of Joe's neck stand on end.

"I don't know," Joe admitted, watching the lights warily. "But I don't like it."

Sophie stepped forward, her expression tense. "They're spirits," she said quietly. "Trapped souls. They're drawn to anyone who enters the mansion."

Mandy took a step back, her eyes wide with fear. "Spirits? You mean like ghosts?"

Sophie nodded. "The Shadow Man feeds on fear, but he also traps souls. Those lights... they're the souls of people who couldn't escape. They're stuck here, wandering the mansion forever."

A cold chill swept over the group at her words. The glowing lights, once strangely mesmerizing, now seemed far more ominous. Joe's heart sank as he realized what they were seeing. These weren't just harmless orbs of light. They were the remnants of people who had been trapped in the mansion, just like Mr. Grimwood had warned them.

"Let's get out of here," Ann said, her voice shaking. "We don't want to end up like them."

The group began to move again, this time with more urgency. But as they continued down the hallway, the lights followed. The orbs hovered just out of reach, bobbing up and down as they floated toward the group. Their glow intensified, casting long, eerie shadows that danced along the walls.

Matt picked up his pace, his voice rising in panic. "Why are they following us?"

Sophie frowned, her brow furrowed in concentration. "They're drawn to fear," she said. "The more afraid we are, the more they're attracted to us."

"Great," Matt muttered, his pace quickening even more. "Well, I'm definitely not calm right now!"

The lights were getting closer now, their glow growing brighter, more intense. The air around them seemed to thrum with energy, and the temperature dropped, making the cold, dark hallway feel even more oppressive.

Joe clenched his fists, trying to stay calm, but his heart was racing. "Stay close," he urged. "Don't let them surround us."

But it was too late. The lights were closing in from all sides, their glow blinding as they circled the group. The orbs bobbed and weaved through the air, casting strange, shifting shadows that made it difficult to tell where the walls of the hallway ended and the spirits began.

Ann's voice trembled as she clutched the book tightly. "They're too close!"

Sophie stepped forward, her face set with determination. "We have to stay calm. If we panic, we'll be trapped."

But the lights were relentless. They swirled around the group, their glowing forms growing brighter and more erratic. The air was thick with energy, and it felt as though the house itself was closing in on them, tightening its grip.

Mandy let out a small cry as one of the lights brushed past her arm. The touch was icy cold, sending a jolt of fear through her body. "It's freezing!"

The others scrambled to move away from the lights, but there was no escape. The orbs seemed to be everywhere, their glowing forms flickering and pulsing like living things. Joe's heart pounded in his chest as he realized they were trapped.

Sophie's voice cut through the chaos. "They're feeding on our fear! We have to push them back!"

Joe glanced at her, desperate for a solution. "How do we do that?"

"Stay together!" Sophie shouted, her voice rising above the growing hum of the lights. "We have to be brave! Don't let them scare you!"

It sounded impossible—how could they stay calm when they were surrounded by the spirits of the dead? But Joe knew Sophie was right. Fear was what gave The Shadow Man and the house their power. If they gave in, they would be trapped just like the souls they were facing now.

"Everyone, hold on!" Joe shouted, trying to rally his friends. "We can't let them win!"

Ann clutched the book to her chest, her face pale but determined. "We're not giving up!"

Mandy, though still trembling with fear, nodded. "We can do this."

Matt took a deep breath, trying to steady himself. "We've made it this far. Let's finish it."

As one, the group formed a tight circle, their flashlights pointing outward. They stood firm, their eyes locked on the glowing orbs of light that surrounded them. The lights pulsed and flickered, growing brighter as if trying to push them into panic.

But this time, they didn't run. They didn't give in to the fear.

The lights seemed to hesitate, their erratic movements slowing. The cold air that had pressed in on them began to lift, and the hallway seemed to stretch out before them once more.

"They're backing off!" Sophie shouted, her voice filled with hope.

Slowly, the lights began to drift away, their glow fading as they retreated into the shadows. The air grew warmer, and the oppressive energy that had filled the hallway began to dissipate. One by one, the orbs of light disappeared, leaving the group standing alone in the dark.

Chapter 9: The Room of Forgotten Toys

The group moved cautiously down the dim hallway, the events of the phantom lights still weighing heavily on their minds. The cold air and oppressive silence of Grimwood Mansion seemed to grow heavier with every step they took, and though the spirits of the trapped souls had retreated, the lingering sense of danger clung to them like a shadow.

Sophie led the way, her flashlight flickering against the worn, cracked walls of the mansion. Joe, Ann, Matt, and Mandy followed closely behind, their expressions a mix of fear and determination. Each of them knew that they were heading deeper into the heart of the mansion, closer to The Shadow Man, and whatever twisted games the house had in store for them next.

"We have to keep moving," Joe said, his voice low and steady. "We're not stopping until we find a way to end this."

Ann glanced down at the old book she carried, *The History of Grimwood Manor.* She had been flipping through the pages whenever she could, but much of the text was too faded to read. What little she could make out described the house's dark history and hinted at the terrible power The Shadow Man had over those who dared enter. "There has to be something in here," she muttered. "Some way to stop him."

"We'll find it," Joe reassured her, though he wasn't entirely sure. He just knew they had to keep going, even if every corner of the mansion seemed like a new trap waiting to spring.

They came to the end of the hallway, where a single door stood slightly ajar. It was smaller than the grand doors they had passed before, and its weathered surface was chipped and cracked with age. There was something unsettling about the door—it didn't seem to belong in the mansion, almost as if it had been forgotten along with whatever was behind it.

Sophie stopped in front of the door, her hand resting on the knob. She hesitated for a moment, her brow furrowed in thought. "I don't remember this room," she said softly. "It wasn't here the last time I came through this hallway."

Matt groaned. "Great. More disappearing and reappearing doors. This house is trying to mess with us again."

"We don't have a choice," Joe said, pushing the door open with a creak. "We need to see what's inside."

The door swung open slowly, revealing a large, dimly lit room. At first glance, it seemed like any other room in the mansion—dust-covered furniture, peeling wallpaper, and an air of neglect. But then, they noticed the toys.

Dozens of old, forgotten toys were scattered across the room. Dolls with cracked porcelain faces, wooden soldiers with chipped paint, stuffed animals that had seen better days. Some toys lay in neat rows, while others were piled in disorganized heaps in the corners of the room. It was as if someone had abandoned them here years ago, leaving them to decay in the darkness.

Mandy stepped inside first, her flashlight sweeping across the room. "Toys? That's... weird."

Ann followed, frowning as she looked around. "What is this place? A nursery?"

Sophie shook her head, her face tense with confusion. "No... I don't think this is a nursery. It feels... wrong."

Matt nudged one of the old stuffed bears with his foot, causing it to topple over. "It's just a bunch of old junk. Creepy, but not dangerous, right?"

But as he spoke, something strange happened. The toys, which had been still and lifeless a moment ago, began to move.

The dolls' heads turned slowly, their glassy eyes locking onto the group. The stuffed animals twitched, their limbs jerking unnaturally as if something was trying to control them. The wooden soldiers shifted, their stiff joints creaking as they stood upright, their painted faces staring blankly ahead.

The room seemed to come alive with the movement of the toys, and a cold, eerie energy filled the air.

Mandy gasped, backing away from a doll whose head had swiveled toward her. "What... what's happening?"

Joe's heart raced as he stepped back, his flashlight trembling in his hand. "It's the house," he said, his voice tight. "It's messing with us again."

Sophie's eyes were wide with fear. "We need to leave. Now."

But before they could move, one of the toys—a jack-in-the-box—suddenly sprang to life. Its lid popped open with a loud, metallic creak, and a grotesque, clownish figure shot out, its painted face twisted into a horrifying grin. The jack-in-the-box lunged toward Ann, its wiry arms reaching out with surprising speed.

"Ann, look out!" Joe shouted, grabbing her arm and pulling her out of the way just in time.

The jack-in-the-box landed where Ann had been standing, its eerie grin frozen in place as it rocked back and forth. But it wasn't the only one. All around them, the toys were stirring, coming to life in unnatural, jerky movements.

The dolls began to crawl across the floor, their tiny hands clawing at the dusty wood. The wooden soldiers marched forward in unison, their stiff legs moving with eerie precision. The stuffed animals shuffled toward the group, their button eyes glinting in the dim light.

Matt backed up until he was pressed against the wall, his eyes wide with terror. "We've gotta get out of here!"

The group scrambled toward the door, but the toys were faster than they had anticipated. The wooden soldiers formed a barricade, their tiny arms raised as if to block the exit. The dolls crawled up the walls and clung to the ceiling, their cracked faces leering down at the group with malevolent glee.

Joe's mind raced as he searched for a way out. The toys were closing in from all sides, their lifeless eyes filled with dark intent. There was no escape—everywhere they turned, another toy was waiting, ready to trap them in the room forever.

"What do we do?" Mandy cried, her voice rising in panic.

Sophie stepped forward, her face set with determination. "We can't let them trap us. We have to fight back!"

"But they're just toys!" Matt shouted, his voice frantic. "How do we fight toys?"

Sophie glanced around the room, her eyes scanning the shelves and piles of forgotten objects. "They're being controlled by the house, just like everything else. We have to break their connection to it."

Ann, clutching the old book tightly, looked down at the text. "Maybe there's something in here. A way to break the spell."

The toys were getting closer, their movements growing more erratic and aggressive. One of the dolls lunged at Joe, its tiny hands clawing at his legs. He kicked it away, but it kept coming, its glassy eyes fixed on him with terrifying determination.

"We don't have time!" Joe shouted, his heart pounding.

Sophie grabbed a nearby chair, lifting it over her head. "Then we make time!"

With a swift motion, she slammed the chair down onto the wooden soldiers blocking the door. The soldiers shattered into pieces, their limbs flying across the room like broken twigs. The other toys hesitated for a moment, their movements slowing as if they were confused.

"Keep going!" Sophie yelled. "Destroy them!"

Joe, Matt, and Mandy grabbed whatever they could—chairs, books, anything heavy enough to break the toys apart. They swung wildly, smashing the dolls, the stuffed animals, and the remaining soldiers into splinters and dust. Ann joined in, her flashlight clutched tightly in one hand as she kicked aside the toys that tried to crawl up her legs.

One by one, the toys fell to the ground, their broken bodies littering the floor. The eerie energy in the room began to fade, and the oppressive feeling that had gripped them since they entered started to lift.

Finally, after what felt like an eternity, the last toy—a battered, one-eyed teddy bear—slumped lifelessly to the floor. The room fell silent.

Breathing heavily, the group stood in the center of the room, surrounded by the wreckage of the forgotten toys. The danger had passed, but the fear still lingered in their hearts.

Chapter 10: The Secret of the Mirror

The group hurried down the hallway, their nerves still frayed from the encounter in the room of forgotten toys. Their breathing was heavy, and the adrenaline from the fight hadn't yet worn off. The silence in Grimwood Mansion pressed down on them, broken only by the occasional creak of the floorboards or the whisper of wind through unseen cracks in the walls.

Ann walked alongside Joe, clutching *The History of Grimwood Manor* tightly to her chest. Her hands trembled as she flipped through the fragile, yellowed pages. "There has to be something in here," she muttered, her voice tense with frustration. "Something we're missing."

"We'll figure it out," Joe said, trying to sound more confident than he felt. He kept his eyes forward, his flashlight cutting through the darkness ahead. "There's always a way."

Sophie, who had taken the lead again, paused at the end of the hallway where another set of stairs descended into the mansion's lower levels. Her face was tight with concentration, and it was clear she was growing more uneasy by the minute. "We're getting closer to the center of the house," she said. "The Shadow Man's power is stronger down here."

Matt, still shaken from the toys, let out a nervous laugh. "I can't wait to see what creepy surprise the house has for us next."

Mandy shot him a look, her voice edged with fear. "I don't even want to think about what else this place is hiding."

As they descended the stairs, the air grew colder. The light from their flashlights seemed to flicker and dim, as though the darkness itself was swallowing it up. The walls, once lined with peeling wallpaper, were now bare and cold, the wood beneath splintered and cracked. It felt as though the mansion was decaying the deeper they went.

At the bottom of the stairs, they found themselves in front of another door. This one was larger than the others they had passed, its surface warped with age. Faint scratches marred the wood, as though something—or someone—had tried to claw their way out.

Sophie placed her hand on the door, hesitating for a moment. "This is where it gets dangerous," she said quietly. "The ballroom is through here. And the mirror."

"The same mirror we saw before?" Joe asked, remembering the eerie, cracked glass that had revealed The Shadow Man's form.

Sophie nodded. "The mirror is where The Shadow Man's power is anchored. If we're going to stop him, we need to understand how it works."

Ann flipped to the back of the book, scanning the faded text. "There's something about the mirror in here. It's tied to the mansion's curse. The original owner of the house—Bartholomew Grimwood—used the mirror in some kind of ritual to trap his enemies. Their souls are bound to the house, and The Shadow Man feeds on them."

Mandy shuddered, her face pale. "So we're dealing with a haunted mirror too?"

"It's more than just haunted," Sophie said, pushing open the door. "The mirror is the source of his power. If we can break it, we can weaken him."

The door groaned as it swung open, revealing the dark expanse of the ballroom once more. The room felt even larger than before, its high ceilings lost in the shadows. The broken chandeliers hung limply, their once-glittering crystals now dull and lifeless. The cracked marble floor was coated in a thin layer of dust, and the heavy curtains on the windows stirred faintly as though moved by an unseen breeze.

But it was the mirror that dominated the room.

The enormous, ornate mirror was mounted on the far wall, its cracked surface gleaming ominously in the dim light. The fractures in the glass seemed to pulse with a faint, ghostly light, as though something on the other side was trying to break through.

Sophie's voice was tense as she stepped into the room. "We have to be careful. The mirror is dangerous."

The group entered cautiously, their flashlights flickering as they moved closer to the mirror. Joe's stomach twisted with unease as he stared at the cracked glass. The last time they had encountered the mirror, The Shadow Man had tried to reach through it, and now, standing this close, Joe could feel the darkness emanating from it.

Ann approached the mirror cautiously, her hands shaking as she held the book in one hand and her flashlight in the other. She scanned the text again, her brow furrowed in concentration. "It says here that the mirror can be used to trap spirits. But it also says that breaking the mirror can release them. If we're not careful, we could unleash something even worse."

Matt, standing a few feet away, let out a nervous laugh. "Great. So if we break it, we might make things even worse?"

Joe stepped forward, his gaze fixed on the mirror. "We don't have a choice. If The Shadow Man is using this mirror to control the house, we have to break his connection to it. We can't let him keep us trapped here."

Sophie nodded, her expression determined. "He's tied to the mirror. If we can weaken his hold, we'll have a chance to escape."

Mandy, who had been silent up until now, glanced around the room nervously. "But how do we break it? It's not like we can just smash it with a rock, right?"

Sophie's eyes darkened as she looked at the mirror. "The mirror is magical. It can't be broken by ordinary means. We need to disrupt the curse—the ritual that keeps it intact."

Ann flipped through the pages of the book, her voice quiet but urgent. "There's something here about a symbol. A protective symbol that can sever the connection between The Shadow Man and the mirror."

She held up the book, showing them a faint, faded drawing of an ancient symbol—a circle with intricate patterns etched inside. "We have to draw this symbol on the mirror. It will disrupt the magic long enough for us to shatter it."

Joe nodded, his heart pounding in his chest. "Then that's what we'll do. Let's find something to draw with."

Sophie quickly scanned the room, her eyes landing on a piece of chalk lying on the floor near one of the broken chandeliers. She grabbed it and handed it to Joe. "Use this. Draw the symbol on the mirror. But hurry. Once we start, The Shadow Man will know what we're doing."

Joe took the chalk, his hand shaking slightly. He approached the mirror, feeling the oppressive weight of the darkness that radiated from it. The cracks in the glass seemed to pulse with energy, and for a moment, Joe thought he saw something moving in the reflection—a shadowy figure watching them from the other side.

He pushed the fear down and began to draw the symbol.

As he traced the lines of the protective circle, the air in the room grew colder. The faint whispers they had heard earlier returned, growing louder with each stroke of the chalk. The shadows in the room seemed to stretch and grow, creeping toward them as if drawn to the mirror.

"Hurry," Sophie urged, her voice tense.

Joe's heart raced as he finished the symbol, the chalk scraping against the cracked glass. The moment the last line was complete, a low, guttural roar echoed through the ballroom.

The mirror began to glow, its surface rippling like water. The cracks in the glass widened, and the faint light that had pulsed from within grew brighter, more erratic.

"He knows," Sophie whispered, her voice filled with dread. "The Shadow Man knows what we're doing."

The room began to shake violently, the chandeliers above them swaying dangerously. The air was thick with energy, and the sound of the mansion groaning under the strain filled their ears. The shadows in the corners of the room surged forward, swirling around the mirror like a dark storm.

Joe stepped back, his eyes locked on the mirror. "We did it. Now we just need to break it."

Matt grabbed a piece of broken wood from the floor and handed it to Joe. "Here. Use this."

With a deep breath, Joe raised the wood above his head and brought it down hard on the mirror. The impact sent a shockwave through the room, and the glass shattered, pieces flying in all directions.

The roar of The Shadow Man filled the room, a deep, angry sound that seemed to shake the very foundation of the mansion. The swirling shadows recoiled, writhing and twisting as if in pain.

For a moment, everything went still. The mirror was broken, its shattered pieces reflecting the dim light from their flashlights. The oppressive energy in the room had lifted, and the air felt lighter, less suffocating.

Chapter 11: The Ghostly Party

The moment the mirror shattered, the mansion seemed to come alive in a way that was even more unnerving than before. The walls groaned and shifted as if the house itself was in pain, and the tremors underfoot became stronger with each passing second. The lights from their flashlights flickered sporadically, casting long, jittery shadows against the warped walls.

"We need to move, now!" Joe urged, his voice barely audible over the strange, guttural sounds echoing through the ballroom.

Sophie led the way, her face set with determination, but her eyes flickered with the fear of what might come next. They'd weakened The Shadow Man by breaking the mirror, but the mansion still had them in its grip. The dark energy in the house pulsed stronger than ever, shifting the very fabric of the rooms and hallways.

Ann clutched the tattered *History of Grimwood Manor* tightly to her chest, her mind racing as she tried to recall any passage that might help them. "I don't know how long we have," she whispered, glancing nervously at the cracks spreading through the walls.

The group pushed open a door at the far end of the ballroom, hoping it would lead them closer to an exit, but what they found was nothing like they expected.

The door opened into a vast room illuminated by the flickering light of hundreds of candles. Chandeliers hung from the ceiling, their crystals gleaming in the soft, golden glow. The room was lavishly decorated with elegant tapestries and intricate patterns that covered the walls and floor. At first glance, it looked like a grand ballroom or banquet hall, untouched by time.

But then, they saw the figures.

Ghostly apparitions filled the room, floating gracefully through the air or standing in clusters, their forms translucent and shimmering. They were dressed in old-fashioned finery—long gowns, ornate suits, and shimmering jewelry—but their faces were pale, their eyes hollow and expressionless.

"It's a party," Mandy whispered, her voice filled with dread. "But... they're all ghosts."

The group froze at the sight. The ghostly figures didn't seem to notice them at first, continuing their silent dance and conversation as if unaware of the group's presence. The eerie waltz of the ghosts created an otherworldly atmosphere, as if the mansion had trapped a moment in time and refused to let it go.

Matt took a hesitant step forward, his flashlight flickering as he scanned the room. "What is this? Some kind of... ghostly celebration?"

Sophie's face was pale as she whispered, "They're the souls The Shadow Man has taken. He traps them here, forcing them to relive the same moment over and over again."

Joe's stomach churned at the thought. These weren't just random ghosts—they were people who had once been alive, just like them. And now, they were prisoners of the mansion, doomed to dance in this eerie, never-ending party for all eternity.

"We can't stay here," Joe said firmly, pulling the group back from the threshold. "We need to find another way out."

But before they could turn around, one of the ghostly figures broke away from the crowd and drifted toward them. It was a woman, her long, elegant gown trailing behind her as she floated across the floor. Her face was blank, her eyes cold and empty, but there was something about her presence that felt deeply unsettling.

Mandy backed away, her eyes wide with fear. "What does she want?"

The ghostly woman stopped a few feet in front of them, her hollow gaze fixed on the group. Slowly, she raised one hand, pointing directly at Joe.

Joe's heart raced as he took a step back. "What is she doing?"

Ann's voice trembled as she said, "I think she's trying to tell us something."

The ghost's lips moved, but no sound came out. Her face twisted in an expression of despair, and the light from the candles flickered violently as if reacting to her presence. Then, suddenly, the air in the room grew colder, and the other ghostly figures began to turn toward the group, their empty eyes locking onto them one by one.

"They can see us," Matt whispered, his voice filled with terror.

As if on cue, the ghosts began to move, drifting toward the group in slow, eerie motions. Their hollow eyes never wavered, and their silent steps echoed in the vast, candlelit room.

"They're coming!" Mandy cried, her voice rising in panic.

Joe's mind raced. They couldn't stay here. Whatever these spirits wanted, it wasn't good. He grabbed Ann's arm, pulling her toward the door at the far end of the room. "Run!"

The group bolted for the door, their footsteps echoing in the silent ballroom as they weaved between the ghostly figures. The apparitions moved faster now, their translucent forms gliding across the floor with unnatural speed. The air was thick with the cold presence of the spirits, and the walls seemed to shimmer as the ghostly energy pulsed through the room.

Sophie led the way, her flashlight barely cutting through the eerie glow of the candlelight. "We have to get out of here before they trap us too!"

As they neared the far end of the room, the ghostly figures closed in around them. One of the spirits—a tall man in a tattered suit—reached out with a skeletal hand, his fingers brushing against Joe's shoulder. The touch sent a wave of icy cold through his body, and for a moment, he felt the pull of the mansion's dark magic trying to drag him into its grasp.

"Joe, keep moving!" Ann shouted, grabbing his hand and yanking him forward.

With a surge of adrenaline, Joe pushed forward, his heart pounding in his chest. The door was just a few feet away, but the ghosts were closing in, their empty eyes filled with a haunting, unspoken sadness.

Matt reached the door first, fumbling with the handle. "It's stuck!"

Sophie rushed to his side, helping him pull on the door. "It's the house! It doesn't want us to leave!"

The ghostly figures were almost upon them now, their cold, translucent hands reaching out to pull the group into their endless, cursed waltz.

"We don't have time!" Mandy cried, her voice filled with desperation.

Joe threw his weight against the door, his hands trembling as he pushed with all his strength. "Come on, we have to get through!"

With one final, desperate push, the door gave way. The group stumbled through the doorway and into another hallway, slamming the door shut behind them. The cold, oppressive presence of the ghosts disappeared, replaced by the silence of the mansion.

They stood there for a moment, gasping for breath, their hearts pounding in their chests. The flickering candlelight from the ballroom cast faint shadows through the cracks in the door, but the ghostly figures did not follow.

Ann, still holding onto *The History of Grimwood Manor,* scanned the pages once more. "The souls we saw—they were victims of The Shadow Man. He's feeding off of them, trapping them in that endless party."

Matt, still shaken, ran a hand through his hair. "We need to figure out how to stop him for good. We can't just keep running."

Chapter 12: The Key to Escape

The hallway they had entered after escaping the ghostly party stretched long and dark before them. The only sound was their footsteps on the creaking floorboards, and the only light came from their flickering flashlights, barely enough to cut through the suffocating gloom. The cold grip of the mansion's supernatural presence weighed heavily on their shoulders, making each step more difficult than the last.

Joe led the group, his face set with determination, but the tension in his body was unmistakable. He glanced over his shoulder at Sophie, who walked close behind him, her expression serious but unshaken. Sophie had been in the mansion longer than the rest of them, and her knowledge was their only advantage against the dark forces that seemed determined to trap them forever.

Ann, clutching *The History of Grimwood Manor* to her chest, muttered to herself as she flipped through the faded pages. She had been searching for something—anything—that might offer a clue about how to defeat The Shadow Man, but so far, the book had offered little more than fragmented histories and half-remembered warnings.

"There's got to be something in here," she murmured, her brow furrowed in concentration.

Matt, who was walking next to her, glanced down at the book. "Anything useful?"

Ann shook her head. "Not yet. I'm looking for something about how to stop him permanently. Breaking the mirror wasn't enough."

Mandy, trailing at the back of the group, spoke up, her voice filled with nervous energy. "You don't think we'll have to face those ghostly people again, do you?"

Joe gave a brief shake of his head, his voice tight. "I don't think so, but I'm not taking any chances."

They continued down the hallway in silence until they reached the end, where another door stood before them. It was a small, unassuming door—nothing like the grand doors they had passed through before. Its surface was plain, the wood cracked and weathered by age. But there was something about it that drew Joe's attention. It was as though the door was important, like it held some secret the mansion was trying to keep hidden.

Sophie stepped forward, her hand resting on the doorknob. "I've never seen this door before," she said quietly. "It wasn't here the last time I passed through this hallway."

Joe glanced at her. "Do you think it's a trap?"

Sophie's expression darkened. "Everything in this house is a trap."

With a nod, Joe motioned for the others to stay back as he slowly pushed the door open. It creaked loudly, and the cold air that rushed out from the room beyond sent a shiver down their spines. The room was small and dimly lit, with narrow beams of moonlight filtering in through a high, broken window. The air inside was musty, and the walls were lined with shelves filled with old, dust-covered objects. At the center of the room, a small wooden table stood, and on it lay a single, rusted key.

The group hesitated for a moment, their eyes fixed on the key.

"A key?" Matt asked, his voice tinged with confusion. "That can't be it, right?"

Sophie took a cautious step forward, her eyes scanning the room for any signs of danger. "I don't know," she said softly. "But we have to check."

Ann moved closer to the shelves, her flashlight revealing stacks of old books, strange trinkets, and small, decaying boxes. The items looked like they had been untouched for decades, maybe even centuries, left to rot in the dark corners of the mansion. "This stuff is ancient," she murmured, picking up one of the books and brushing away the thick layer of dust. "But why would they leave a key out in the open like that?"

Joe approached the table cautiously, his flashlight trained on the key. There was something eerie about it—something that made the hair on the back of his neck stand on end. It was as though the key was waiting for them, as if it had been left there on purpose.

"Do you think this is the key to escape?" Mandy asked, her voice trembling.

Sophie stepped forward, her expression thoughtful. "It's possible. The mansion's magic is tied to symbols, rituals, and artifacts. A key like this could be part of whatever keeps the house under The Shadow Man's control."

Joe reached out, his hand hovering over the key. "But what if it's another trap?"

Sophie shook her head. "It might be. But we don't have a choice. If this key can get us out, we have to take it."

Taking a deep breath, Joe picked up the key. It was cold to the touch, its metal worn and rusted from age. As soon as his fingers closed around it, a strange sensation washed over him. The air in the room seemed to shift, and the walls trembled slightly as if the mansion itself had noticed the key's removal.

"Something's happening," Ann said, her eyes widening as the room seemed to grow darker.

Before they could react, the door behind them slammed shut with a deafening bang. The walls began to creak and groan, and the air in the room grew thick with the familiar oppressive energy of the house's dark magic.

"We have to get out of here!" Matt shouted, rushing toward the door.

But when he grabbed the doorknob and tried to pull it open, the door wouldn't budge. It was sealed tight, trapping them inside.

Sophie's voice was tense as she scanned the room. "It's the house. It's trying to stop us from leaving with the key."

Joe's heart raced as he looked around, trying to find another way out. The shelves rattled, and the objects on them began to shift and shake as though disturbed by an invisible force. The room was coming alive, and it wasn't going to let them go without a fight.

"There has to be another exit!" Joe shouted, his eyes scanning the walls for any sign of a hidden door or passage.

Ann flipped through the book, her voice frantic as she searched for a clue. "There's nothing in here about a key! I don't know what to do!"

Suddenly, the walls began to ripple and warp, and a low, guttural growl echoed through the room. The temperature plummeted, and the shadows in the corners of the room seemed to deepen, stretching out toward the group.

"It's him," Sophie whispered, her face pale. "The Shadow Man. He's coming."

Joe's grip tightened on the key as the growling grew louder. They had to get out—now.

"Look!" Mandy pointed to a small window high up on the far wall. It was narrow, barely large enough for them to squeeze through, but it was their only option.

"We can make it through there!" Joe said, rushing toward the window. "Matt, give me a boost!"

Matt hurried over and clasped his hands together, creating a foothold for Joe. With a quick push, Joe climbed up to the window, using the cracked and crumbling walls to steady himself. He peered out through the broken glass, feeling the cool night air on his face.

"It leads outside!" Joe shouted, a wave of relief washing over him. "We can climb out!"

One by one, the group climbed up to the window, their hearts pounding as the growling grew louder and more menacing. The shadows in the room were closing in, creeping toward them like dark tendrils.

Sophie was the last to climb up, her face tense with concentration as she pushed herself through the narrow window. Just as she was about to pull herself out, a cold hand shot out from the shadows, grabbing her ankle.

Sophie gasped, her eyes wide with fear as she kicked at the shadowy hand. "It's trying to pull me back!"

Joe reached down, grabbing her arm and pulling her up with all his strength. "We've got you! Hang on!"

With one final tug, Sophie broke free of the shadow's grasp and scrambled through the window. The group tumbled onto the overgrown grass outside, gasping for breath.

They had made it out of the room. But the mansion wasn't done with them yet.

Chapter 13: The Library of Shadows

The cold night air offered only a brief moment of respite from the suffocating atmosphere of the mansion. Joe, Sophie, Ann, Matt, and Mandy stood outside for a few precious seconds, catching their breath after narrowly escaping the room and the dark forces within. The rusted key Joe held in his hand felt heavier than before, as though it carried the weight of the mansion's curse. He glanced at it, the metal cool against his skin, and a question gnawed at his mind: What lock did it open?

"We've weakened The Shadow Man, but we're not done," Sophie said, her voice resolute but tinged with exhaustion. "This key is important. We just need to find where it fits."

Ann flipped through *The History of Grimwood Manor*, her brow furrowed as she scanned the faded pages. "There's not much in here about the key itself, but there's a section about the mansion's library. It talks about powerful magic and dark rituals being performed there. Maybe that's where we'll find the lock."

Joe nodded, gripping the key tightly. "It's our best shot. Let's head to the library."

With renewed determination, the group re-entered the mansion through a side entrance, bracing themselves for whatever new horrors awaited them. The interior of the house was as cold and unsettling as ever. The walls seemed to pulse with a dark energy, and the shadows stretched and twisted in unnatural ways, as if they were alive and watching.

They moved quickly, navigating the twisting hallways and staircases with Sophie's guidance. As they descended deeper into the mansion, the air grew thicker and more oppressive. The creaking of the floorboards beneath their feet echoed in the otherwise silent corridors, reminding them of how alive the mansion felt. It was as though the house was reacting to their every move, waiting for the right moment to strike.

Finally, they reached a large, ornate door. Faded gold leaf adorned the edges, and the intricate carvings of strange, mythical creatures seemed to shift as the light from their flashlights played across them. Above the door, an old wooden sign read: *The Grimwood Library.*

"This is it," Sophie said softly, her voice barely above a whisper. "The Library of Shadows."

Joe took a deep breath and pushed open the heavy door. It groaned in protest, but eventually swung inward, revealing a massive, dimly lit library. Shelves upon shelves of ancient books lined the walls, stretching up toward the high, vaulted ceiling. Dust hung in the air, illuminated by the narrow beams of moonlight that filtered through the grimy, stained-glass windows.

The room was eerily quiet, the only sound the faint rustling of their footsteps on the old, worn carpet. The library was massive, much larger than they had anticipated, and the sheer number of books was overwhelming. But there was something else—something darker that lingered just beneath the surface. The air felt thick with the residue of centuries-old magic, and the shadows between the shelves seemed deeper than they should have been.

"We have to find the lock," Joe said, his voice steady but tense. "Spread out, but don't go too far."

The group split up, moving cautiously between the towering shelves. Joe kept his flashlight trained ahead, searching for anything that might resemble a lock or hidden door. The deeper he ventured into the library, the more oppressive the atmosphere became. It was as if the room itself was watching him, waiting for him to make a mistake.

Ann and Mandy moved through the rows of books, their flashlights casting long shadows on the walls. Ann's eyes scanned the titles of the dusty tomes, hoping to find something that might give them a clue. "This place feels like a maze," she whispered. "How are we supposed to find anything in here?"

Mandy shook her head, her voice trembling slightly. "I don't know. But I don't like the feeling I'm getting."

As they continued their search, something shifted in the darkness. The shadows between the shelves seemed to ripple and move, as though something was lurking just out of sight. The air grew colder, and the faint sound of whispering filled the room. It was soft at first, barely audible, but it grew louder with each passing second.

"Do you hear that?" Matt asked, his voice filled with unease as he stepped closer to Joe. "It sounds like... whispering."

Joe nodded, his jaw clenched. "I hear it. Stay alert."

The whispering intensified, filling the room with a low, insistent murmur that seemed to come from every direction at once. The shadows between the bookshelves shifted again, growing darker, thicker, as if they were alive.

Suddenly, a book flew off one of the shelves and landed on the floor with a loud thud. Ann jumped, her heart racing as she shone her flashlight toward the source of the noise. "What was that?"

Before anyone could answer, more books began to fall from the shelves, one after another, until the entire library was filled with the deafening sound of books crashing to the floor. The whispering grew louder, more urgent, and the shadows began to move in unnatural ways, swirling and twisting like living things.

"We need to move!" Sophie shouted, her eyes wide with fear. "It's the house! It's trying to trap us!"

The group rushed toward the center of the library, dodging the falling books and the thickening shadows. The darkness seemed to reach out for them, tendrils of black smoke curling through the air like grasping hands. Joe's heart pounded in his chest as he clutched the key tightly in his hand, knowing that they were running out of time.

"There!" Ann shouted, pointing to the far end of the room where a small, ornate chest sat on a pedestal.

Joe's eyes locked onto the chest. It was old, with intricate carvings etched into its surface, and there was a small keyhole in the center. "That has to be it!"

With the whispering growing louder and the shadows closing in around them, the group sprinted toward the chest. Joe skidded to a stop in front of it, fumbling with the key as his hands shook. The air around them was filled with the oppressive weight of the mansion's magic, and it felt as though the walls were closing in.

"Hurry!" Mandy cried, glancing over her shoulder as the shadows writhed and twisted, forming into shapes that looked almost human.

Joe jammed the key into the lock, twisting it with all his strength. For a moment, nothing happened, and fear shot through him like a bolt of lightning. But then, with a loud click, the chest unlocked, and the lid slowly creaked open.

Inside the chest was a small, ornate dagger. The blade gleamed in the dim light, and the hilt was encrusted with strange symbols that pulsed with an eerie glow. The moment Joe touched the dagger, the whispering stopped, and the shadows seemed to recoil.

Sophie stepped forward, her eyes fixed on the dagger. "That's it. That's what we need to defeat The Shadow Man."

Joe held the dagger tightly, feeling the power that radiated from it. "This is how we stop him."

Ann glanced around the library, her eyes filled with apprehension. "We need to get out of here before the house fights back again."

The group turned and made their way toward the exit, their hearts pounding as the oppressive energy in the room seemed to lessen with each step. But just as they reached the door, the shadows surged forward once more, swirling and twisting into a dark, human-like figure.

It was The Shadow Man.

His tall, dark form loomed before them, his glowing red eyes fixed on the group. His voice echoed through the library, low and menacing. "You cannot escape. The house is mine, and so are you."

Joe's grip tightened on the dagger. "We're not afraid of you anymore."

The Shadow Man's form twisted and shifted, his laughter filling the room like the sound of grinding stone. "You will be."

Without warning, the shadows lashed out, swirling around the group with terrifying speed. The bookshelves toppled over, and the walls seemed to pulse with the dark magic that filled the mansion. The air was thick with the weight of The Shadow Man's power, and the group found themselves surrounded by an impenetrable darkness.

But Joe didn't hesitate. He raised the dagger high, the symbols on the hilt glowing brighter as they pulsed with energy. With a fierce determination, he plunged the dagger into the shadowy figure.

The moment the blade made contact, The Shadow Man let out a terrible, inhuman scream. The darkness around them shuddered, and the shadows writhed and twisted as if in agony. The oppressive energy that had filled the room began to dissipate, and the figure of The Shadow Man started to fade.

The library fell silent.

The Shadow Man was gone.

Joe let out a breath he hadn't realized he was holding, his heart still racing. The dagger in his hand was warm, pulsing with the faint remnants of the magic that had defeated The Shadow Man.

Chapter 14: The History of the Shadow Man

The oppressive weight of the mansion seemed to lift slightly after the encounter in the Library of Shadows. Joe, Sophie, Ann, Matt, and Mandy moved cautiously down the hallway, the dagger that had weakened The Shadow Man now securely in Joe's grip. Though they had won a battle, they knew the war was far from over. The mansion still pulsed with dark energy, and The Shadow Man's influence lingered in every shadow, in every creaking floorboard.

Ann clutched *The History of Grimwood Manor* close as she hurried beside Joe. "There has to be more in this book," she murmured, flipping through the old pages. "We've uncovered pieces of The Shadow Man's power, but we don't know the full story yet."

Joe nodded, though his mind was racing with a dozen other concerns. The closer they got to the heart of the mansion, the more they realized how twisted and dangerous it was. They had found the dagger, but the key to fully defeating The Shadow Man still eluded them. And Joe couldn't shake the feeling that time was running out.

"Does it say anything about where The Shadow Man came from?" Mandy asked, glancing nervously at the dark corners of the hallway as they passed. "How did he even get this kind of power?"

Ann frowned as she scanned a page near the back of the book. "There's something here... I think this might be it. It talks about Bartholomew Grimwood—the original owner of the mansion. He's the one who became The Shadow Man."

Matt leaned in closer. "What does it say? How did he end up like that?"

Ann hesitated for a moment, then began to read aloud, her voice echoing in the cold, silent hallway. "Bartholomew Grimwood was a wealthy man, but his wealth wasn't enough. He was obsessed with power and immortality. He spent years studying dark magic, rituals that could grant him control over life and death."

As Ann read, the group continued down the winding hallways, the mansion seemingly growing darker with every step.

"The book says that Bartholomew discovered an ancient ritual—one that could trap souls and bind them to a place forever. He wanted to become immortal, to live forever in his mansion, ruling over those whose souls he had trapped. But something went wrong."

Joe's grip on the dagger tightened as they walked. "What went wrong?"

Ann turned the page, her brow furrowed. "It says that during the ritual, Bartholomew lost control of the magic. Instead of becoming immortal, his soul was torn from his body and bound to the house itself. He became a shadow, a twisted version of the man he once was. That's how The Shadow Man was born."

Sophie's face was pale as she listened. "So he's not just a ghost. He's something worse—he's part of the house."

"Exactly," Ann replied. "His power comes from the souls he's trapped. The more fear he creates, the stronger he becomes. And the longer people stay in the house, the more likely they are to become trapped, just like the others we saw at the party."

Mandy shuddered, her voice trembling. "So all those ghosts... they were his victims?"

Ann nodded. "Yes. And if we don't stop him, we'll become his next victims."

Joe's stomach churned as the weight of the situation settled over him. The Shadow Man wasn't just some ghost haunting the mansion—he was the mansion. He had used dark magic to bind his soul to the house, and now he fed on fear and trapped souls to sustain his power.

"But there has to be a way to stop him," Matt said, his voice tinged with desperation. "We can't let him win."

Ann flipped through the book's final pages, her eyes scanning the text for anything that might help. "The book mentions that the ritual that created The Shadow Man can be undone. But it requires more than just breaking the mirror or using the dagger. We need to sever his connection to the mansion."

Sophie's eyes narrowed. "How do we do that?"

"There's a way," Ann said, her voice steady. "Bartholomew's soul is tied to a specific place in the mansion—his study. It was where he performed the ritual. If we go there, we can use the dagger to break his connection to the house."

Joe's heart pounded in his chest as he processed Ann's words. The study—of course. It all came back to the place where Bartholomew Grimwood had performed the ritual, the place where he had made his fatal mistake. If they could reach the study, they might have a chance to undo the curse and destroy The Shadow Man for good.

"Then that's where we need to go," Joe said, determination flooding his voice. "We'll find the study, use the dagger, and end this."

The group quickened their pace, their footsteps echoing through the dark, twisting hallways. The mansion seemed to groan in response to their resolve, the walls creaking and the air growing colder. It was as if the house itself was aware of their plan—and it wasn't going to make it easy for them.

Sophie led them through a series of corridors, her flashlight flickering as they moved deeper into the heart of the mansion. The tension in the air was thick, and each corner they turned felt like it could be the start of another trap. But they pressed on, knowing that the study was their last hope.

After what felt like hours of navigating the maze-like halls, they finally reached a set of large, imposing doors. The wood was dark and polished, with intricate carvings of strange symbols etched into its surface. Above the doors, a faded plaque read: *The Grimwood Study.*

"This is it," Sophie whispered, her voice filled with a mix of fear and determination. "Bartholomew's study."

Joe glanced at the others, taking a deep breath. "We're ready. Let's end this."

With trembling hands, Joe pushed the doors open. The room beyond was dark and foreboding, filled with the remnants of a once-lavish study. Shelves lined the walls, filled with dusty tomes and strange, arcane objects. A massive desk sat in the center of the room, and behind it, a large, cracked window overlooked the mansion's overgrown gardens.

But it was the figure standing at the far end of the room that made Joe's heart stop.

The Shadow Man was there, his tall, dark form looming in the dim light. His glowing red eyes burned with malice as he stepped forward, his voice a low, echoing growl. "You think you can stop me? This house is mine, and you are nothing but fleeting shadows in my domain."

Joe's grip on the dagger tightened. "We're not afraid of you anymore. This ends now."

The Shadow Man's form flickered, the shadows around him twisting and writhing like living things. "You cannot destroy me. I am the house. I am everything here. You belong to me."

Ann stepped forward, the book open in her hands. "We know what you are. You're not invincible, Bartholomew. You're just a man who made a mistake—and now it's time to pay the price."

The Shadow Man let out a chilling laugh, his red eyes flashing. "You are fools. I have lived for centuries, feeding on the fear of those who dare to enter my domain. You cannot defeat me."

But Joe didn't hesitate. He raised the dagger high, its symbols glowing with an eerie light. "This is for everyone you've trapped here."

With a surge of strength, Joe plunged the dagger into the floor at the center of the study. The moment the blade made contact, the room exploded with light. The shadows recoiled, and The Shadow Man let out a terrible scream that shook the very walls of the mansion.

The air in the room grew thick with energy, and the ground beneath their feet trembled. The Shadow Man's form twisted and writhed, his red eyes glowing brighter as he struggled to maintain his hold on the house.

"No!" he roared, his voice filled with fury and desperation. "You cannot defeat me!"

But the light from the dagger continued to grow, pulsing with a brilliant, blinding energy. The walls of the study began to crack, and the shadows that had once filled the room were torn apart by the power of the ritual.

As the light consumed him, The Shadow Man's form dissolved, his twisted, dark figure disappearing into nothingness. His final scream echoed through the mansion, and then there was silence.

Chapter 15: The Shadow Man Revealed

The air inside Grimwood Mansion grew colder with every step the group took. Joe, Sophie, Ann, Matt, and Mandy moved cautiously through the twisting hallways, the weight of the house's dark energy pressing down on them. The oppressive feeling that something terrible was waiting for them lingered in the air, making each step more difficult than the last. They had come far, but the mansion was still alive, still watching their every move.

The dagger that Joe had used to weaken The Shadow Man felt heavy in his hand, as though it carried the burden of the souls trapped within the house. His heart pounded in his chest, and the closer they got to the heart of the mansion, the more his fear threatened to overwhelm him.

"This is it," Sophie said quietly, her voice filled with tension. "We're getting close. The Shadow Man is waiting for us."

Ann clutched *The History of Grimwood Manor* tightly, her eyes scanning the dark corners of the hallway. "We need to be ready. He's more dangerous now that we've weakened his connection to the house."

Mandy's voice trembled as she whispered, "What if we can't stop him? What if he's too strong?"

Sophie glanced at her, her face grim. "We can stop him. We have to."

As they turned a corner, the hallway opened up into a vast, dark room. It was unlike any other room they had seen in the mansion—a large, empty space with towering ceilings and walls shrouded in darkness. The air was colder here, and the shadows seemed to pulse with a life of their own. The flickering beams of their flashlights barely penetrated the gloom, and an overwhelming sense of dread settled over the group.

Joe's grip tightened on the dagger. "He's here."

And then, without warning, the darkness in the room seemed to shift. A low, menacing growl echoed through the air, and the shadows at the far end of the room began to swirl and twist. Slowly, a figure emerged from the darkness—tall, ominous, and shrouded in a swirling cloak of black mist. His eyes glowed with an eerie red light, and his form seemed to flicker in and out of reality, as though he wasn't entirely bound to this world.

It was The Shadow Man.

The air grew colder as he stepped forward, his hollow eyes locking onto the group with a malevolent intensity. His voice echoed through the room, low and sinister. "You thought you could escape me. But you cannot. This house is mine, and you will never leave."

Joe's heart raced as The Shadow Man's presence filled the room. His shadowy figure towered over them, his long, bony fingers stretching out toward the group as if he were already claiming them as his own.

Ann took a step back, her face pale with fear. "What do we do now? He's too powerful."

Sophie's eyes were locked on The Shadow Man, her expression filled with a mix of fear and determination. "There's something you all need to know," she said quietly, her voice trembling slightly. "I wasn't always just a visitor here. I've been trapped in this mansion for a long time... by him."

The group stared at her in shock. "What do you mean?" Joe asked, his voice filled with confusion. "How long?"

Sophie's eyes never left The Shadow Man as she spoke. "I was just like you—caught in the mansion's web. It was years ago... I don't even remember how long. I came here with a group of friends, just like you, thinking we could explore an old, haunted house for fun. But The Shadow Man trapped us. One by one, my friends were taken, their souls bound to the house. I've been searching for a way to defeat him ever since."

Mandy's voice was filled with disbelief. "You've been here for years?"

Sophie nodded, her expression pained. "Yes. I've seen countless others fall into his trap, just like we almost did. But I've been looking for a way to break the curse, to end his hold over the mansion. And now... now we have a chance."

The Shadow Man's low, mocking laughter filled the room, his form flickering as he moved closer. "You think you can defeat me, Sophie? You have tried before—and you have failed every time."

Joe stepped forward, his grip on the dagger tightening. "We're not afraid of you anymore. You can't keep us here."

The Shadow Man's eyes gleamed with malice as he sneered. "You think this dagger will save you? You are mere mortals, weak and insignificant. I am the master of this house. I am eternal."

Sophie took a deep breath, her voice steady as she addressed the group. "The Shadow Man's power comes from fear. He feeds on it, grows stronger with every soul he traps. But if we stand together—if we face him without fear—we can break his hold."

Matt's voice shook as he glanced at Sophie. "But how? He's stronger than ever."

Sophie looked at Joe, her eyes filled with determination. "We have the dagger. It's not just a weapon—it's a symbol of resistance, of hope. Bartholomew Grimwood was a man once, just like us. His power is rooted in the ritual he performed, but he is still vulnerable. We can stop him, but we have to be brave."

The Shadow Man hissed, his form growing darker as he moved toward them. "You cannot resist me! This house is my domain, and you are nothing but shadows in my grasp!"

Joe's heart pounded in his chest as The Shadow Man loomed before them, his dark, swirling form filling the room. But as fear threatened to overwhelm him, Joe remembered Sophie's words. The Shadow Man thrived on fear—but they had a weapon. They had the dagger, and they had each other.

With a surge of determination, Joe raised the dagger high. "We're not afraid of you anymore, Bartholomew Grimwood. You don't control us."

The Shadow Man's eyes flared with anger, and the shadows around him twisted violently. "You are fools! You will suffer for your defiance!"

But as The Shadow Man lashed out, Sophie stepped forward, her voice ringing with defiance. "No, Bartholomew. It's you who will fall. You've been trapped in this house for too long. Your time is over."

The group stood together, their resolve unshaken. The darkness around them swirled and pulsed, but they didn't back down. Joe gripped the dagger tightly, feeling its warmth pulse through his hand, and he knew what had to be done.

With a cry, Joe lunged forward, driving the dagger toward The Shadow Man's dark, twisted form. The moment the blade made contact, the room exploded with light. The shadows recoiled, and The Shadow Man let out a terrible scream, his form twisting and writhing as if in agony.

The air around them shimmered with energy, and the walls of the mansion seemed to shake as The Shadow Man's hold over the house began to weaken.

"No!" he roared, his voice filled with fury and desperation. "You cannot defeat me!"

But the light from the dagger continued to grow, pulsing with a brilliant, blinding energy. The shadows around The Shadow Man dissolved, and his dark, twisted figure began to fade.

With one final scream, The Shadow Man vanished into nothingness, leaving only silence behind.

Chapter 16: The Trick Room

The defeat of the Shadow Man left an eerie silence hanging over the group, but the oppressive energy of Grimwood Mansion still lingered. As they continued through the labyrinthine hallways, it became clear that the house wasn't letting go of them just yet. Despite the victory, each of them felt the weight of the mansion's dark presence like a heavy shroud, and they knew their journey was far from over.

"We need to keep moving," Joe said, his voice quiet but firm. The dagger in his hand, now drained of its radiant energy, felt heavier than ever. They had defeated the Shadow Man, but the mansion still thrived, twisted with dark magic. They couldn't afford to rest, not yet.

Sophie nodded. "The house still has more tricks up its sleeve. We're not safe."

Ann clutched *The History of Grimwood Manor*, her fingers running over its ancient, worn cover. "We have to find the exit before it's too late. There has to be something in here that can help us."

The group pressed on, walking in a tight formation as they ventured deeper into the mansion. The walls seemed to close in around them, the corridors narrower and darker than before. Cold drafts of air swept past, carrying faint whispers that made Mandy shiver.

After a few minutes of tense silence, they reached a door at the end of a long, narrow hallway. It was different from the others they had encountered—large and intricately carved with swirling patterns. The design seemed to shift under their gaze, warping and twisting, as if the door itself was alive.

"This doesn't feel right," Matt said, his voice low, a tremor in his tone. "Do we really want to go in there?"

"We don't have a choice," Joe replied, swallowing hard as he reached for the door handle. "We need to keep moving."

With a deep breath, he pushed the door open. The room beyond was vast and shrouded in darkness, but as they stepped inside, the door slammed shut behind them with a loud bang, causing everyone to jump.

Suddenly, the room was illuminated by an unnatural glow, and the group found themselves surrounded by mirrors. Dozens, maybe hundreds, of floor-to-ceiling mirrors stretched out in every direction. Each one reflected their images, but there was something wrong with the reflections—they were distorted, twisted versions of themselves, with wide, fearful eyes and expressions of terror.

Mandy gasped. "What is this place?"

"It's another one of the mansion's tricks," Sophie said grimly, her eyes scanning the room. "A room of illusions, meant to trap us."

As they stood frozen, the mirrors began to shift. Their reflections no longer mirrored their movements. Instead, each mirror showed a nightmare version of themselves, acting out their greatest fears.

Joe's mirror showed him trapped in a crumbling building, the walls collapsing around him, crushing him. His breaths grew shallow as he watched his reflection pound against the walls, desperately trying to escape.

Ann's mirror revealed her lost in a dark, endless forest, calling out for help, but no one responded. Her voice cracked in fear, her reflection wandering further into the woods as shadows closed in.

Matt's mirror depicted him standing on a stage in front of a huge, jeering crowd, unable to speak. The pressure of their judgment weighed on him, and his knees buckled under the strain.

Mandy stood frozen before her mirror, watching in horror as shadows swirled around her reflection, whispering her name, trying to pull her into the darkness.

Sophie's reflection, however, was the most haunting. Her mirror showed her standing alone in the mansion, watching as her friends disappeared one by one, leaving her trapped and alone, forever.

"The mirrors are feeding on our fears," Sophie said, her voice barely above a whisper. "If we don't face them, we'll be trapped here."

Joe tore his eyes away from the terrifying reflection and clenched his fists. "We can't let them control us. It's just an illusion. We've faced worse than this."

Ann took a deep breath, her hands trembling as she stepped closer to her mirror. "You're not real," she said, her voice shaking but resolute. "I won't let you scare me."

As she spoke the words, her reflection flickered, the dark forest beginning to fade. Encouraged, she pressed on. "You're not real," she repeated, louder this time. "You can't control me."

With that, her reflection shattered, the mirror cracking and splintering into a thousand pieces. Ann stepped back, gasping in relief as the shards fell to the floor, disappearing into the darkness.

Mandy followed her lead, her voice quivering but strong. "You're not real. You're just shadows. You can't hurt me."

Her reflection wavered, the swirling shadows receding until they vanished completely. The mirror cracked, shattering just like Ann's, and Mandy let out a breath she hadn't realized she was holding.

Matt, still shaken by the vision of the jeering crowd, stood frozen for a moment longer. But as he glanced at his friends, he found the strength to face his fear. "You're not real," he said, his voice steadying. "I won't let you control me."

The reflection of the crowd began to fade, their mocking laughter growing quieter until it was nothing more than a faint echo. The mirror splintered, and Matt took a step back, relief washing over him.

Joe, his heart still pounding from the vision of the collapsing building, closed his eyes and took a deep breath. "This isn't real," he whispered, forcing himself to stay calm. "It's just a trick."

When he opened his eyes again, his reflection was flickering, the walls of the crumbling building beginning to fade. With a final surge of determination, Joe stepped forward, touching the mirror's surface. The glass shattered beneath his fingers, and the nightmare disappeared.

Now, only Sophie remained. Her reflection still showed her standing alone, her friends vanishing into the darkness. She hesitated, fear flickering in her eyes.

"You're not alone, Sophie," Joe said softly, stepping toward her. "We're here. We won't leave you."

Sophie's eyes filled with tears, but she nodded, her voice trembling as she faced her reflection. "You're not real," she whispered. "I'm not alone."

The reflection flickered, the empty mansion fading away as the real Sophie stood tall, her resolve strengthening. The mirror shattered, and the illusion was broken.

The room around them seemed to shift, the oppressive energy lifting as the last mirror fell to pieces. The eerie glow dimmed, and the door at the far end of the room creaked open.

The group stepped through the open door, leaving the Trick Room behind. But they knew the mansion still had more challenges in store for them. The house had tried to break them with fear, but they had faced it head-on and survived.

Chapter 17: The Hall of Time

The door creaked as Joe pushed it open, revealing a long, narrow hallway beyond. A chill ran down his spine the moment he stepped inside. The hallway was different from the rest of the mansion—eerily quiet, save for a rhythmic ticking that echoed through the air. As the others followed, their footsteps seemed to melt into the constant ticking that surrounded them.

The walls were lined with clocks—hundreds of them, in all shapes and sizes. Grandfather clocks, ornate wall clocks, small pocket watches suspended in glass cases—each one ticked at a different pace, creating a chaotic symphony of time. Some clocks moved too fast, their hands spinning wildly, while others moved so slowly that it was hard to tell if they were moving at all. Some had stopped altogether, frozen in place.

Ann stepped closer to one of the clocks, her brow furrowed. "This is... strange. I don't like this place."

"Time," Sophie said softly, her voice heavy with tension. "This is the Hall of Time. I've heard about it before."

Joe shot her a questioning glance. "The Hall of Time? What does that mean?"

Sophie's eyes scanned the walls, her expression grim. "Time doesn't work the same here. It bends, twists... You can get lost in it. If we don't get out of here quickly, we might be trapped forever."

Matt's eyes widened as he stared at the clocks, his breath quickening. "Trapped forever? In a time loop?"

Sophie nodded slowly. "Yes. The mansion uses this place to trap people in loops, keeping them here indefinitely. We need to find the exit and get out before it's too late."

A palpable sense of urgency swept through the group as her words sank in. The ticking of the clocks grew louder in Joe's ears, and the distorted rhythm of the room made him feel dizzy. He gripped the dagger tightly, though it no longer glowed with the power it once had.

"We should move," Joe said, his voice firm. "The sooner we're out of here, the better."

They moved forward cautiously, the hallway stretching out in front of them. The further they walked, the more the clocks seemed to shift. Joe glanced at his watch, but its hands spun erratically, offering no sense of time. He tried to focus on the path ahead, but it felt like they were walking in circles.

Ann slowed her pace, glancing nervously at the clocks. "It feels like we're not getting anywhere."

Mandy shivered, her eyes darting from one clock to the next. "How do we even know which direction we're supposed to go?"

Sophie pressed her lips together, her eyes narrowing as she studied the hallway. "It's hard to tell. This place is designed to confuse us, to make time feel meaningless."

Joe clenched his fists, frustration building in his chest. "We just have to keep moving. There has to be an end somewhere."

But as they continued down the hallway, time itself seemed to warp. Moments stretched out, making seconds feel like minutes, while other moments blurred by in the blink of an eye. The clocks on the walls became a dizzying blur, their erratic ticking making it impossible to gauge how long they had been walking.

"We're stuck," Matt said, his voice laced with panic. "We're stuck in a time loop, aren't we?"

"No," Sophie said sharply. "We're not stuck. Not yet. We just have to keep our heads straight. Don't let the mansion get to you."

Ann's voice trembled. "But how do we know? We've been walking for so long, and it feels like we're just going in circles."

Joe's mind raced. They needed a way to ground themselves, a way to tell if they were actually making progress. But with every step, the hallway seemed to stretch on, the clocks ticking faster and faster, warping time around them. He could feel it slipping through his fingers, like sand in an hourglass.

Suddenly, a loud, booming chime echoed through the hallway. The sound reverberated off the walls, making everyone jump. Joe spun around, his heart racing, and realized the source of the noise—it was one of the larger clocks, a massive grandfather clock near the end of the hall.

The hands on the clock had reached the top—midnight.

Sophie's eyes widened in alarm. "We're running out of time. If we don't find the exit before midnight strikes, we'll be trapped."

Joe felt a surge of adrenaline. They needed to move—now. He glanced around frantically, searching for any sign of an exit, but the hallway seemed endless, the clocks ticking louder and faster with each passing second.

"We're close!" Sophie shouted, pointing toward a faint glow in the distance. "There's something up ahead!"

Joe squinted, his heart pounding in his chest. She was right—there was a dim light coming from the end of the hallway, barely visible through the warping air. It had to be the way out.

"Let's go!" Joe shouted, breaking into a sprint.

The others followed, their footsteps pounding against the floor as they raced toward the light. The air around them seemed to shimmer, the ticking of the clocks growing deafening. Joe's legs burned as he pushed himself harder, the sense of time slipping away growing stronger with every step.

As they ran, the hallway seemed to stretch and distort, the exit appearing farther away with each passing moment. Joe's heart raced as he felt the pressure building—time was running out.

"Faster!" Matt urged, his voice barely audible over the noise.

The clocks struck again—another chime, louder this time, shaking the walls. Midnight was approaching. Joe could feel it in his bones.

"We're almost there!" Sophie cried, her eyes locked on the glowing exit.

With every ounce of strength they had, they surged forward, the light growing brighter as they neared the end of the hallway. Joe's lungs burned, his legs felt like they were about to give out, but he didn't stop. They couldn't stop.

Finally, they reached the doorway. Joe skidded to a halt and reached for the handle, yanking the door open. A blast of cold air hit them as they tumbled through the door, collapsing onto the floor in the room beyond.

For a moment, everything was still. The ticking had stopped. The deafening noise of the clocks had vanished, leaving only a faint ringing in their ears. Joe lay on his back, gasping for breath, his chest heaving with exhaustion. He could feel the cold stone floor beneath him and the steady rhythm of his heart as it slowed down.

"We... we made it," Ann whispered, her voice trembling with relief.

Sophie sat up slowly, her face pale but her eyes steady. "We did. Just in time."

Joe rolled onto his side, staring back at the door they had just come through. The faint glow of the hallway had disappeared, leaving only darkness. The Hall of Time was behind them, but the weight of its strange, warping energy still clung to him.

Matt let out a shaky laugh. "That was close. Way too close."

Joe sat up, rubbing his temples as he tried to steady his thoughts. They had made it out, but they had come dangerously close to being trapped. Midnight had been seconds away, and the thought of what might have happened if they hadn't reached the door in time sent a chill down his spine.

"We need to keep moving," Joe said quietly, his voice hoarse. "We're not out yet."

The group slowly got to their feet, each of them still shaken by the experience but determined to keep going. The clocks, the warping time, the pressure of the mansion's twisted reality—all of it had tried to break them, but they had made it through.

Chapter 18: Matt's Disappearance

The cold, heavy air clung to the group as they caught their breath from the mad dash through the Hall of Time. Every step they took deeper into Grimwood Mansion seemed to pull them further into its twisted, haunted heart. Though they had narrowly escaped the disorienting labyrinth of clocks, the sense of impending doom hadn't left them.

The hallway they now found themselves in was narrow and dimly lit by the flickering light of old lanterns hanging crookedly on the walls. The stone floor beneath them creaked and groaned with every footfall, as though the house itself was complaining about their presence.

"We have to be close to the exit by now," Joe muttered, glancing nervously down the hallway.

Sophie shook her head, her eyes filled with both fear and determination. "No. The mansion still has more in store for us. I can feel it. The Shadow Man may be gone, but this house... it doesn't want us to leave."

Ann was flipping through *The History of Grimwood Manor*, her fingers tracing the ancient text. She squinted at the faded pages. "It says here that the mansion can change. It warps and shifts as it pleases. The closer we get to the exit, the more it'll fight us."

Matt, ever the optimist, tried to lighten the mood. "Well, as long as the walls don't start moving, we should be okay, right?" His laugh was shaky, betraying his attempt to cover the fear clawing at his insides.

"Don't joke about that," Mandy whispered. "At this point, I wouldn't be surprised if this place had moving walls."

They continued down the hallway, each of them hyper-aware of their surroundings, every creak and distant whisper sending a shiver down their spines. Joe led the way, his grip still tight on the dagger, even though its power seemed to have faded. Ann and Mandy stayed close behind, their eyes darting around nervously. Sophie lingered at the back, her face pale but focused, as though she were trying to sense something just beyond the edge of her awareness.

As they walked, the tension in the air grew thicker. Joe couldn't shake the feeling that something was terribly wrong. The hallway seemed to stretch longer and longer, and there was no sign of the exit. Just endless shadows.

Suddenly, there was a loud thud behind them.

"Matt?" Joe called, spinning around. But when he turned, Matt was gone.

Mandy's scream cut through the silence, her eyes wide with terror. "Where is he?! He was right here! He was just right here!"

Joe's heart raced as he ran back toward where Matt had been walking only moments ago. The hallway was empty—no sign of a struggle, no sound, no trace of Matt at all.

"Matt!" Joe shouted, his voice echoing down the long, empty corridor.

Ann gripped her book tightly, her face pale with fear. "This can't be happening," she whispered. "Where did he go?"

Sophie stepped forward, her expression dark and serious. "The mansion took him."

Joe turned to her, his pulse pounding in his ears. "What do you mean 'the mansion took him'?"

"The Shadow Man might be gone, but the house still has its own power. It can manipulate space, and it knows we're close to escaping. It's trying to trap us—and it's taken Matt," Sophie explained, her voice steady despite the rising panic around them.

Mandy's eyes filled with tears. "We have to find him! We can't leave without him!"

Sophie nodded firmly. "We will. But we don't have much time. The sun will rise soon, and if we're still here when it does, we'll all be trapped. We have to find Matt quickly."

Joe's stomach twisted with fear. He looked around the hallway, searching for any clue, any sign of where Matt could have gone. But the corridor remained unnervingly silent.

"Where would the mansion take him?" Ann asked, her voice trembling.

Sophie's face darkened, and she glanced down the hallway. "I think I know. The Shadow Man's lair. It's deep within the mansion, hidden in the darkest part of the house. If Matt was taken anywhere, it would be there."

Joe felt a cold chill crawl up his spine. The thought of venturing deeper into the mansion, toward the heart of its malevolent energy, made him want to turn and run the other way. But Matt was one of them—his best friend—and they couldn't leave him behind.

"We have to go," Joe said firmly. "We'll find him. No matter what."

Sophie led the way, guiding the group through a series of twisting corridors and narrow staircases. As they moved, the mansion seemed to grow darker, colder. The walls groaned and creaked, and every shadow seemed to reach for them, clawing at their heels as they hurried forward.

"The mansion is trying to confuse us," Sophie whispered as they entered a particularly long corridor. "It's trying to lead us away from Matt. Stay close. Don't get separated."

The hallway stretched on endlessly, the floor beneath their feet shifting with every step. At times, it felt as though the walls themselves were closing in, bending and twisting in ways that shouldn't have been possible. Ann clutched her book tightly, murmuring to herself, as though the words of *The History of Grimwood Manor* could offer some protection.

Mandy was close to tears, her hands trembling as she followed behind Joe. "I just want this to be over," she whispered. "I want to go home."

"We're going to get home," Joe assured her, though his own voice wavered. "We just need to find Matt first."

As they moved further into the mansion's depths, the air grew colder. The flickering lights that lined the hallway dimmed, casting long, sinister shadows that danced along the walls. Joe could feel the mansion's oppressive energy pressing down on him, making it harder to breathe.

Suddenly, they reached a large, ornate door at the end of the hallway. It was old and weathered, covered in intricate carvings of twisting vines and skulls. A chill ran down Joe's spine as he stared at it.

"This is it," Sophie said quietly. "The Shadow Man's lair."

Joe swallowed hard, his heart pounding in his chest. He glanced back at the others, seeing the fear in their eyes. They were all terrified, but they knew they had to press on.

Without another word, Joe pushed open the door. It creaked loudly, the sound echoing through the hallway. Beyond the door was a massive chamber, shrouded in darkness. The air was thick and cold, and a sense of dread washed over them as they stepped inside.

The room was vast, with high, vaulted ceilings and walls lined with ancient, crumbling bookshelves. A faint glow illuminated the far end of the chamber, where a dark figure stood—Matt. He was slumped against a stone altar, his face pale, his eyes closed.

"Matt!" Joe shouted, running toward him.

But as he neared the altar, a voice echoed through the chamber—low, cold, and filled with malice.

"You thought you could defeat me?" the voice hissed. "You thought you could leave?"

Joe's heart skipped a beat. The voice wasn't coming from any one direction—it surrounded them, reverberating through the walls.

Sophie's eyes widened in horror. "No. It can't be."

Before they could react, the shadows in the chamber began to shift and twist, coalescing into a familiar figure—the Shadow Man. His form flickered and wavered, as though he were not entirely bound to the physical world, but his presence was undeniable.

"You may have weakened me," the Shadow Man hissed, his hollow eyes glowing faintly. "But you will never leave this house."

Joe felt his breath catch in his throat. The Shadow Man's form was less solid than before, but he was still there—still part of the mansion.

Sophie stepped forward, her voice steady but filled with fury. "You're not in control anymore. We destroyed you."

The Shadow Man's laughter echoed through the chamber. "You may have broken my connection, but I am this house. And you... will never escape."

Joe gritted his teeth, his grip tightening on the dagger. "We're taking Matt, and we're leaving."

The Shadow Man's form flickered, his voice growing darker. "You can try."

The shadows around them began to move as the group braced themselves for the final confrontation. They had come too far, fought too hard, to give up now.

Chapter 19: The Shadow Man's Lair

The cold, oppressive air inside the Shadow Man's lair hung thick, suffocating the courage Joe and the others had tried to summon. The room was vast, filled with darkness that seemed to swallow their presence whole. At the center, bathed in a dim, ghostly light, stood Matt, trapped inside a cage made of swirling shadows. His face was pale, eyes half-closed, as if the mansion had drained his energy, slowly feeding on his very soul.

"Matt!" Joe's voice echoed through the cavernous room as he raced forward, his heart pounding in his chest. He grabbed the bars of the cage, but the moment his fingers touched them, an icy pain shot through him. Joe recoiled, shaking out his stinging hands.

"Stay back!" Sophie called out, her eyes locked on the dark form that hovered just beyond the cage—The Shadow Man. His shape was not fully solid, more a mass of shifting darkness with hollow, glowing red eyes. His presence filled the room, a malevolent force that oozed power and despair.

"You thought you could escape me," The Shadow Man hissed, his voice as cold as the room itself. He stepped forward, his form flickering as though it could barely hold together. "You thought you could destroy me. But as long as this house stands, *I* stand."

Ann, clutching *The History of Grimwood Manor* to her chest, stepped closer to the cage, her eyes darting between Matt and the ominous figure looming above them. "Let him go!" she demanded, her voice trembling but firm. "We know your power is weakened. You can't hold us here forever."

The Shadow Man's laughter filled the chamber, a cruel, chilling sound that made the hair on the back of Joe's neck stand up. "You are bold," he said, his voice echoing from the walls, "but foolish. My power may be weaker, but I still control this house. I *am* this house."

He moved closer to Matt's cage, his shadowy fingers brushing the bars lightly. The cage pulsed with an eerie light, and Matt groaned softly inside, his head lolling to the side as though he were barely conscious.

"You want your friend," The Shadow Man said, his voice low and dangerous. "But everything has a price."

Joe clenched his fists, anger boiling up inside him. "We're not playing your games anymore," he said through gritted teeth. "We're leaving here, all of us—including Matt."

The Shadow Man's eyes gleamed with dark amusement. "Are you willing to make a deal, then?" His form swirled around the cage, a cloud of darkness and mist. "You may leave this mansion... but I will keep him." He gestured toward Matt, his voice dripping with malice. "Leave now, and the rest of you will be free. Or stay... and you will all be trapped forever."

Mandy gasped, stepping back in horror. "No... no, we can't leave him. We won't leave him!" Her voice cracked, her fear palpable.

Sophie, her face pale but determined, stepped forward. "We're not bargaining with you," she said, her eyes locked on the Shadow Man. "We've faced you before, and we're not afraid anymore. You don't control us."

The Shadow Man's laughter echoed again, but there was something different about it this time—a flicker of frustration, a crack in his façade. "Bravery," he sneered. "Foolish bravery. But I will give you one last chance. Walk out of this room now, and I will let you live. Stay, and you will never leave."

Joe tightened his grip on the dagger, its cold hilt reminding him of the battle they had fought before. The Shadow Man was weaker, that much was clear. But even in his weakened state, he was still dangerous. The air around them pulsed with dark energy, and the walls seemed to close in, as though the mansion itself was tightening its grip.

"We're not leaving without Matt," Joe said, his voice firm and steady. "If you think we're afraid of you, you're wrong."

The Shadow Man's form shifted, swirling closer to the group, his red eyes burning with fury. "You *should* be afraid," he hissed. "I have taken hundreds before you—children, adults, all foolish enough to wander into my domain. They thought they could defeat me too. And now their souls belong to me."

"Not today," Sophie said sharply. She reached into her pocket and pulled out a small, rusted key—the same key they had found earlier in the mansion. "We know how to stop you."

The Shadow Man recoiled slightly, his form flickering in the dim light. "You think a simple key will defeat me?"

"This isn't just a key," Sophie said, stepping forward. "It's part of the ritual that gave you power in the first place, isn't it? You bound your soul to this mansion, trapping yourself here. But that means you're vulnerable. We can break the connection."

Ann stepped forward, her fingers tracing the lines of the ancient book. "It's all in here," she said, flipping open the pages. "Your greed, your desire for eternal life—that's what trapped you in this house. But you're still bound by the same rules."

The Shadow Man let out a low growl, his form flickering violently as he lunged toward the group. "You know nothing! I am eternal! I *am* this house!"

Joe raised the dagger, positioning himself between the Shadow Man and his friends. "Maybe you were once," he said, his voice filled with determination. "But not anymore."

As The Shadow Man surged forward, the room darkened, the shadows around them swirling violently. But Joe stood firm, raising the dagger in defense. Sophie held out the key, her eyes narrowing with focus as she began to recite the words she had memorized from the book—words of power, words that could break the Shadow Man's hold over the mansion.

The air in the room crackled with energy, and the walls seemed to shake as Sophie's voice grew stronger. The Shadow Man let out a furious scream, his form flickering wildly as he tried to attack, but Joe swung the dagger, slicing through the shadows with a burst of light. The blade, though weakened, still held enough power to push him back.

"You can't stop me!" The Shadow Man roared, his voice filled with fury. "I am eternal!"

But as Sophie recited the final words of the incantation, the key in her hand began to glow. A blinding light filled the room, and The Shadow Man let out a scream of pure rage. His form twisted and writhed, the shadows around him collapsing as the connection between him and the mansion began to break.

"No!" The Shadow Man howled, his voice fading as his form dissolved into darkness. "You cannot defeat me!"

With a final, ear-piercing scream, The Shadow Man's figure disintegrated, his dark energy dissipating into nothingness. The room fell silent, the oppressive energy lifting as the mansion's hold over them began to break.

Joe stumbled forward, rushing to Matt's side as the shadowy cage around him dissolved. Matt collapsed into Joe's arms, weak but alive.

Chapter 20: The Final Battle

The air inside Grimwood Mansion seemed to ripple with darkness as the group stood together in the aftermath of their confrontation with the Shadow Man. Though they had weakened him, his presence still lingered, filling the mansion with an oppressive weight that made every breath feel heavy. The walls groaned, shifting unnaturally as though the house itself was alive, trying to force them back into its shadowy grasp.

Joe wiped the sweat from his brow, his heart still pounding from the intense confrontation. Matt leaned heavily against him, weak but conscious, his eyes fluttering open as he slowly regained his strength. Ann hovered nearby, clutching *The History of Grimwood Manor* in one hand and the glowing key in the other. Sophie stood at Joe's side, her face pale but determined, her gaze fixed on the swirling darkness that still hung in the air where the Shadow Man had vanished moments before.

"Is he really gone?" Mandy asked, her voice shaking as she glanced nervously around the room.

Sophie shook her head, her expression grim. "Not yet. We've weakened him, but he's not finished. He's still tied to this house, and he'll try to trap us again."

The floor beneath their feet trembled slightly, a low rumble vibrating through the stone as if the mansion itself was reacting to Sophie's words. The Shadow Man may have been forced to retreat, but his presence still poisoned the very foundation of Grimwood Mansion. The group knew that this wasn't over.

"We need to move," Joe said, his voice steady despite the fear gnawing at him. "He'll come back, and when he does, we have to be ready."

Ann, flipping through the pages of *The History of Grimwood Manor*, found her voice again. "There's something in here," she muttered, scanning the ancient text. "Something about the final confrontation. It says here that his connection to the mansion can only be fully severed if we destroy the source of his power."

"The source?" Joe asked, his brow furrowing. "What's his source?"

Ann's finger hovered over a passage in the book. "The ritual he performed centuries ago—the one that bound his soul to this house—was fueled by his greed. It says he tied his life force to an object in the mansion, something that represents his greed and desire for power."

Joe felt a chill run down his spine. "So, if we destroy that object, we can destroy him for good?"

Sophie nodded slowly. "Yes. But finding it won't be easy. The mansion will try to stop us."

Matt, still leaning on Joe for support, managed to speak. "Whatever it is, we don't have much time. This place... it feels like it's falling apart."

Sophie's eyes darkened as she looked around the crumbling room. "The mansion's connected to him. If we don't stop him, we'll all be trapped here."

Joe tightened his grip on the dagger, his resolve hardening. "We'll stop him. Together."

With the weight of their decision pressing down on them, the group quickly gathered themselves and set off. The mansion seemed to resist their every step, the floors buckling and shifting beneath them as they moved through the twisting corridors. Shadows danced along the walls, whispering threats that seemed to echo from every corner. The house was alive, and it didn't want to let them go.

"This way," Sophie called out, leading the group down a narrow hallway that spiraled deeper into the mansion's depths. The further they descended, the colder the air became, and the more oppressive the atmosphere grew.

As they reached the base of the mansion, they found themselves standing before a massive set of iron doors. Ancient and covered in rust, the doors were engraved with swirling patterns that seemed to pulse with dark energy. Behind them, Joe knew, lay the heart of the mansion—the place where the Shadow Man had performed his dark ritual so many years ago.

"This is it," Sophie whispered, her voice barely audible above the howling wind that seemed to rise from the very walls. "This is where it all began."

Joe stepped forward, pushing the doors open with a grunt. The moment the doors creaked apart, a blast of cold air hit them, and they were met with a scene that made Joe's blood run cold.

The room beyond was vast, its ceiling lost in shadows. At the center of the chamber stood a large, ornate altar, covered in thick cobwebs and surrounded by flickering candles. And at the base of the altar lay the object they had been searching for—a dark, twisted artifact that pulsed with an eerie red glow. It was a mirror, small and ornate, but its surface shimmered with dark energy, swirling like liquid smoke. This was the object that held the Shadow Man's power.

"There," Ann said, pointing toward the mirror. "That's it. That's what's keeping him alive."

But before they could move, the shadows in the room began to swirl violently, coalescing into a familiar figure—the Shadow Man. He emerged from the darkness, his form barely holding together as though he were made of smoke and mist. But his eyes—those glowing red eyes—were filled with fury.

"You think you can destroy me?" The Shadow Man hissed, his voice echoing through the chamber. "You are nothing. This house is mine. I am eternal!"

Joe felt a surge of adrenaline as the Shadow Man lunged toward them, his shadowy form twisting through the air like a storm of darkness. Without thinking, Joe raised the dagger, swinging it toward the Shadow Man with all his strength. The blade connected with the swirling mass of shadows, and a burst of light exploded from the dagger, sending the Shadow Man reeling back with a furious scream.

"Now!" Sophie shouted, her voice filled with urgency. "We need to destroy the mirror!"

Ann sprinted toward the altar, holding the glowing key tightly in her hand. The Shadow Man let out a deafening roar, his form twisting and writhing as he tried to stop her, but Joe and Sophie stood their ground, blocking his path. Sophie raised her hand, chanting the incantation she had memorized from the book, her voice ringing with power as she called upon the ancient words that would weaken him further.

The room shook violently as the Shadow Man lashed out, his dark energy swirling around them like a whirlwind. But Joe didn't falter. He swung the dagger again, the blade slicing through the shadows and forcing the Shadow Man to retreat.

Ann reached the altar, her heart pounding in her chest as she thrust the key into the mirror. The moment the key touched the surface, the mirror pulsed with a blinding light, and a terrible scream filled the air as the Shadow Man let out a cry of pure rage.

"No!" he roared, his form disintegrating before their eyes. "You cannot defeat me! I am eternal!"

But it was too late. The mirror shattered, its surface cracking and splintering as the dark energy that had sustained the Shadow Man was destroyed. The room erupted with light, and the shadows dissolved into nothingness, leaving behind only silence.

The group stood in stunned silence, their hearts racing as the last remnants of the Shadow Man's power faded into the ether. The mansion, once alive with darkness, now felt still—its oppressive energy gone.

Chapter 21: Defeating the Shadow Man

The moment the mirror shattered and the Shadow Man's form dissolved into darkness, the group had felt a brief, fleeting sense of relief. But that relief quickly evaporated as the walls around them trembled and the floor beneath them cracked like the surface of thinning ice. The mansion, once held together by the Shadow Man's dark power, was beginning to collapse in on itself.

"We need to move!" Joe shouted, his voice barely audible over the groaning walls and the rumbling beneath their feet. Dust and debris fell from the ceiling, and the floor buckled as if the house was coming apart at the seams.

Sophie, her eyes wide with panic but still focused, grabbed Ann's arm. "It's not over. I can feel it. He's still here, clinging to the mansion. He's not done with us yet."

Ann clutched the key that had shattered the mirror, her heart racing. "How can he still be here? We destroyed his connection!"

Sophie shook her head, her brow furrowed with determination. "The ritual bound him to the house, but we didn't sever his source of power entirely. He's been feeding off the mansion and its wealth for centuries. His greed... it's what gives him strength."

Joe, panting from the exertion of holding the dagger high, turned to face the others. "So, if his greed is his weakness, we can use that against him."

Matt, who had regained some of his strength after being freed from the cage, took a step forward. "How? The mansion's falling apart, and he's still lurking in the shadows. We don't have time."

A dark, hollow voice filled the air, cold and venomous. "Time is *exactly* what you no longer have."

The group froze as the Shadow Man's form began to materialize once more, rising out of the shadows like a creature born of darkness itself. He was weaker now, his shape barely holding together, but the malevolent energy surrounding him was still palpable. His glowing red eyes fixed on the group, seething with fury.

"You thought you could defeat me," he hissed, his voice echoing from the crumbling walls. "But I am eternal. You are mere children, playing at something far beyond your understanding."

Joe's grip on the dagger tightened, and he stepped forward, placing himself between the Shadow Man and the rest of the group. "We know what you are now. You're nothing but a greedy, power-hungry soul, clinging to a mansion that's falling apart. You don't control us anymore."

The Shadow Man laughed, a hollow, chilling sound that reverberated through the collapsing room. "Greed? Power? You speak of things you cannot comprehend. This house and everything in it *belongs* to me. And now... so do you."

As the ground beneath them trembled violently, a plan began to form in Sophie's mind. She looked at Joe, then at the others. "He's right—he thrives on greed. But if we give him exactly what he wants, we can distract him long enough to trap him."

Ann, still clutching *The History of Grimwood Manor*, nodded in understanding. "An illusion. We give him what he desires most—riches, power—something so grand that he won't be able to resist."

Joe's eyes widened. "We make him think he's won."

Sophie turned to the others, her voice filled with urgency. "Ann, you still have the key, and we have the pieces of the shattered mirror. If we create the illusion of endless wealth, we can trap him inside the mirror's reflection. It's risky, but it's our only shot."

Mandy, her face pale but resolute, glanced around at the disintegrating room. "But how do we create an illusion strong enough to fool him?"

Sophie bit her lip, thinking quickly. "We'll use the mansion itself. We've seen how it warps and shifts—it's already filled with illusions. We just need to tap into that power."

The Shadow Man's form flickered in the shadows, his patience wearing thin. "Your time is up," he growled, beginning to surge toward them.

Joe, without hesitating, raised the dagger and shouted, "Show us the riches of Grimwood Mansion! Show us the wealth of the man who thought he could live forever!"

The air around them shimmered as if in response to Joe's command. The mansion, sensing the desire for wealth, began to change. The walls, once crumbling and covered in dust, shimmered with gold. The floor beneath their feet transformed into polished marble, and the chandeliers above glowed with dazzling light. Piles of gold coins, glittering jewels, and priceless artifacts appeared, strewn across the room like the treasures of a long-lost kingdom.

The Shadow Man froze, his red eyes glowing brighter as he took in the scene before him. His twisted form seemed to strengthen, feeding off the illusion of riches that surrounded him.

"Yes," he whispered, his voice thick with greed. "This... this is mine."

Ann, who had been holding the shattered pieces of the mirror, stepped forward, her hands trembling but steady. "You want it all? It's yours."

With a flick of her wrist, she threw the pieces of the mirror into the air. They caught the shimmering light of the illusion, reflecting the gold and jewels back at the Shadow Man. For a moment, it seemed as though the entire room had turned into a gleaming palace, filled with endless wealth.

The Shadow Man, utterly captivated by the illusion, reached out with his long, shadowy fingers, grasping at the riches before him. His eyes burned with desire, his greed overwhelming every other thought.

Joe gave Sophie a nod. "Now!"

Sophie raised the key, her voice steady as she recited the final words from *The History of Grimwood Manor*. "Bound by your greed, by your desire for power, you are trapped within this mirror! Return to the shadows from whence you came!"

The pieces of the mirror, still floating in the air, began to swirl around the Shadow Man. His form flickered, confusion and rage spreading across his face as he realized what was happening. He tried to pull away, but the pull of the mirror's magic was too strong.

"No!" the Shadow Man screamed, his voice filled with fury. "You cannot trap me! I am eternal!"

But it was too late. The pieces of the mirror coalesced around him, forming a swirling vortex of light and shadow. The illusion of riches faded, and the Shadow Man's form was drawn into the mirror, his screams echoing through the room as he was trapped within its glassy surface.

With a final, ear-piercing wail, the Shadow Man disappeared into the mirror, leaving behind only silence.

For a moment, the group stood in stunned disbelief, their hearts pounding as they stared at the now still room. The mirror, once shattered, was whole again, its surface smooth and reflective. But instead of showing their reflections, it held the swirling shadow of the Shadow Man, trapped forever in his own greed.

"We... we did it," Joe whispered, his voice hoarse.

Sophie lowered the key, her hands shaking from the adrenaline. "We trapped him," she said softly. "He's gone. For good this time."

But before they could celebrate, the ground beneath them shook violently. The mansion, no longer sustained by the Shadow Man's power, was collapsing. The walls groaned and cracked, and pieces of the ceiling began to fall around them.

"We have to get out of here!" Matt shouted, his voice filled with urgency.

Joe grabbed the mirror, tucking it safely under his arm as they turned and sprinted toward the exit. The floor buckled beneath them, and the walls began to crumble as they raced through the twisting corridors of Grimwood Mansion, the sound of destruction all around them.

The final battle was over, but the mansion wasn't done with them yet. They had to escape before the entire house came crashing down.

Chapter 22: The Escape

The ground beneath their feet trembled violently, sending shudders through the walls of Grimwood Mansion. The air was filled with a deafening groan as the ancient structure, no longer bound by the dark power of the Shadow Man, began to crumble in on itself. The group, still catching their breath from the battle, stood frozen for a moment, eyes wide as the realization hit them—this place was falling apart, and they had to escape.

"We need to get out now!" Joe shouted, gripping the mirror tightly in his arms, the swirling shadow of the trapped Shadow Man still visible inside. Dust rained down from the ceiling, and large chunks of debris were beginning to fall around them.

Sophie spun toward the exit, her voice filled with urgency. "The front door! We have to make it before the house collapses!"

Matt, still weak but filled with adrenaline, staggered to his feet. "Let's move!" His voice was hoarse, but the fear and determination in his eyes were clear.

Without another word, the group dashed toward the nearest doorway, the sound of the mansion's walls groaning louder with each step. The floor beneath them cracked and shifted, as if the house itself was fighting to hold itself together. Ann, clutching *The History of Grimwood Manor*, led the way with Joe close behind, still gripping the mirror that held the Shadow Man's essence.

The hallway ahead was dimly lit by flickering candles that sputtered in the swirling dust. The air was thick, making it harder to breathe with each passing moment. Chunks of plaster and wood fell from the ceiling, crashing to the ground with loud, echoing thuds.

"Watch out!" Mandy screamed as a massive wooden beam cracked and fell from above, smashing onto the floor just inches from her feet.

Joe grabbed her arm, pulling her to safety. "We have to keep moving! It's all coming down!"

They rounded a corner, the walls shaking violently, sending paintings crashing to the ground. The mansion, once filled with eerie whispers and the oppressive weight of the Shadow Man's presence, now seemed to be screaming in pain as it crumbled. It was as though the very soul of the house was disintegrating, leaving nothing but chaos in its wake.

"The stairs!" Sophie called, pointing to the grand staircase up ahead. But the staircase, once a majestic, if ominous, centerpiece of the mansion, was now broken and splintered. Half of it had already collapsed, leaving the group no choice but to carefully navigate their way down the remaining steps.

"Careful!" Joe yelled as they hurried down, dodging falling debris. His heart raced in his chest as the house continued to shake around them.

As they descended, the floor beneath them creaked and groaned ominously, threatening to give way at any moment. The chandelier that had once hung high above the foyer now swung wildly, the crystals clinking together like wind chimes in a storm.

Ann stumbled on a loose step but caught herself, her breath coming in sharp, terrified gasps. "We're almost there!" she cried, the front door finally visible at the far end of the foyer.

But just as they reached the bottom of the staircase, a deafening crack split the air. The chandelier, its chain weakened by the tremors, broke free and plummeted toward them.

"Look out!" Matt shouted, diving out of the way as the massive fixture crashed to the ground, shattering into a million pieces and sending shards of crystal skittering across the floor.

Joe and Sophie helped pull Ann to her feet, their faces streaked with dust and fear. "Come on!" Sophie urged. "We're so close!"

They raced toward the front door, the walls around them cracking open as if the house was being torn apart by invisible hands. Every step felt like a race against time, the ground quaking beneath their feet.

The front door was just ahead now, its once-foreboding presence now the only thing standing between them and freedom. The heavy wooden door, with its intricate carvings and ancient iron hinges, creaked and groaned as if it were alive, as if it were deciding whether to open or keep them trapped inside forever.

Joe's heart pounded in his chest as he reached for the door handle, his hand slick with sweat. He pulled with all his strength, but the door wouldn't budge. "It's stuck!" he shouted, panic rising in his throat. "It won't open!"

"No!" Ann cried, her eyes wide with fear. "We can't be trapped here! Not now!"

Sophie stepped forward, her face set with determination. "Stand back!" She raised the key—the same one they had used to break the Shadow Man's hold on the mirror—and thrust it into the door's ancient keyhole.

For a moment, nothing happened. The house continued to shake violently, pieces of the ceiling falling around them, and it seemed as though they would be buried alive beneath the weight of the collapsing mansion.

But then, with a loud *click*, the door's lock disengaged.

The door creaked open slowly, just enough for the group to see the dark night sky beyond. A gust of cool air rushed in, filling their lungs with the fresh, crisp scent of freedom.

"It's open!" Joe yelled, his voice filled with relief.

They didn't need any more encouragement. One by one, they squeezed through the narrow opening, dodging falling debris as the mansion groaned and shifted behind them. The ground beneath them heaved as they stumbled out onto the front porch, their bodies covered in dust and grime.

Just as Joe, the last to leave, pulled himself through the doorway, the house gave one final, thunderous roar. The front door slammed shut behind him with a deafening *boom*, and the entire mansion seemed to implode. The walls caved in, the roof collapsed inward, and the towering structure that had loomed over them for so long began to disintegrate into rubble.

They ran across the yard, the sound of the house collapsing filling the air behind them. With every step, the mansion fell further into ruin, its once-imposing frame now reduced to a pile of debris.

Finally, they reached the edge of the property, their breaths coming in ragged gasps. They turned just in time to see the last remnants of Grimwood Mansion crumble into dust. Where the ancient house had stood for centuries, there was now nothing but a smoking ruin, the dark energy that had once filled it gone forever.

The group stood in stunned silence, staring at the remains of the mansion. The weight of everything they had been through settled over them like a heavy blanket. It was over—the Shadow Man, the mansion, all of it. They had survived.

The dust began to settle as a faint glow appeared on the horizon. The sun, slowly rising in the distance, cast a soft, golden light over the land. The first rays of dawn touched their faces, and for the first time in what felt like an eternity, they felt warmth.

Chapter 23: A Halloween to Remember

The early morning air was crisp, cool, and filled with the scent of dew-covered grass as the group stood just outside the ruins of Grimwood Mansion. The sun had fully risen, casting a soft golden glow over the landscape, but even its warmth couldn't entirely banish the cold chill that lingered from their harrowing ordeal. They were all covered in dust and dirt, their clothes torn and their faces streaked with exhaustion. But despite their battered appearance, there was a palpable sense of relief in the air—they had survived.

The ruins of the mansion still loomed behind them, but something strange was happening. As they watched, the debris seemed to shimmer in the soft morning light, and a faint mist began to rise from the crumbled stones. It was almost as if the house itself was fading away, dissolving into the air like a memory too old to hold its shape.

Joe stood at the front of the group, the weight of the mirror in his hands lighter now that the Shadow Man had been trapped within it. He stared at the crumbling remains of Grimwood Mansion, feeling a sense of closure wash over him. For the first time since stepping foot on the property, the oppressive, dark energy of the mansion had disappeared. The place felt empty now, devoid of the malevolent force that had haunted it for so long.

"Look," Mandy whispered, pointing toward the ruins.

The mist that had risen from the mansion's remains was swirling now, twisting in the air like a thick fog. It moved unnaturally, coiling in on itself until it formed a hazy silhouette. Slowly, the shape became clearer, and out of the mist stepped a familiar figure—Mr. Grimwood.

The old man looked just as he had when they first met him: tall, with a weathered face and sharp eyes that seemed to see straight through them. He wore his tattered coat, the brim of his hat casting a shadow over his brow. But this time, there was something different about him. His eyes, once filled with mystery and warning, now held a softness, almost a sense of peace.

"Mr. Grimwood," Ann whispered, her voice barely audible in the still morning air.

He stepped forward, a slight smile tugging at the corners of his lips. "You did it," he said, his voice steady but filled with quiet pride. "You freed the house."

Joe, still holding the mirror that contained the Shadow Man's essence, took a step toward him. "What do you mean, we freed the house? Who are you really, Mr. Grimwood?"

The old man let out a soft chuckle, his eyes crinkling at the edges. "I suppose it's time you knew the truth. I've been watching over Grimwood Mansion for a very long time—far longer than anyone in town realizes. I was once its protector, long before the Shadow Man twisted its halls into a prison of darkness."

Ann furrowed her brow, her curiosity piqued despite her exhaustion. "A protector? How?"

Mr. Grimwood glanced back at the ruins, his expression somber. "The mansion was once a place of great power, a place where magic could be harnessed for good. But it was also a place of temptation. Bartholomew Grimwood—the man you know as the Shadow Man—was once a part of this house's legacy. He was consumed by greed, driven mad by his desire for eternal life and riches. He performed a ritual that bound his soul to the mansion, turning it into a prison for all who entered."

"So you've been here all this time?" Sophie asked, stepping forward. "Watching over the mansion, waiting for someone to break the curse?"

Mr. Grimwood nodded slowly. "Yes. I couldn't enter the mansion myself—the curse kept me out, just as it trapped anyone who ventured inside. But I could guide those brave enough to try, warn them of the dangers. I've seen countless people come and go, most of them never making it out."

Matt, still visibly shaken but more himself now, frowned. "Why didn't you tell us all of this when we first met you? Why all the riddles and warnings?"

Mr. Grimwood's expression softened. "I've learned over the years that too much information can be overwhelming. People need to discover the truth for themselves. If I had told you everything from the beginning, you might not have believed me—or worse, you might have been too afraid to enter at all. But you were different. I saw something in you—courage, determination, and the strength to do what no one else could."

Joe glanced down at the mirror in his hands, watching the faint, swirling shadow inside it. "So now that we've trapped him, is it over? Is the Shadow Man gone for good?"

Mr. Grimwood nodded. "Yes. You've done what needed to be done. By trapping him in the mirror, you've severed his connection to the mansion. His greed was his undoing, just as it has been for centuries. He's powerless now, unable to escape."

Ann let out a sigh of relief, the tension finally leaving her shoulders. "So the mansion... it's free?"

Mr. Grimwood turned to look at the dissolving ruins behind them. "The curse is lifted. The mansion is returning to the earth now, fading away as it was meant to. It will no longer haunt this land, and its dark history will be forgotten. In time, nature will reclaim this place, and all that will remain are stories."

Mandy, who had been quietly watching the scene unfold, finally spoke. "So that's it? We're free to go home?"

Mr. Grimwood smiled warmly. "Yes, you're free. You've done something incredible tonight—something that many others tried and failed to do. You've broken the curse, and for that, I am eternally grateful."

The group stood in silence for a moment, letting the weight of Mr. Grimwood's words sink in. The sun had fully risen now, bathing the landscape in warm light. The ruins of the mansion continued to dissolve into mist, as if the very essence of the house was being washed away by the morning light. It was a strange, surreal sight—watching the place that had been the source of so much terror simply disappear before their eyes.

Joe turned back to Mr. Grimwood, a question still lingering in his mind. "What will happen to you now? Now that the mansion is gone?"

The old man's smile faded slightly, replaced with a wistful expression. "My time here is over as well. With the Shadow Man defeated and the house no longer cursed, my duty as protector has come to an end."

Sophie frowned, stepping closer to him. "But where will you go?"

Mr. Grimwood gave a gentle shrug. "I'm not sure. But I have a feeling I'll find peace now, just as the house will. My purpose here is complete, and that's all I've ever wanted."

For a moment, none of them spoke. There was something both sad and hopeful in Mr. Grimwood's words—a sense of finality, but also a sense of release. He had been tied to Grimwood Mansion for so long, trapped just as much as the souls that had been claimed by the Shadow Man. But now, he could finally be free.

As the last remnants of the mansion disappeared into the mist, Mr. Grimwood stepped back, his figure beginning to fade along with the ruins. "Take care, all of you," he said softly, his voice growing fainter. "You've done more than you know."

And with that, he was gone, dissolving into the morning mist just as the mansion had. The group stood in stunned silence for a long moment, watching the empty space where both Mr. Grimwood and the mansion had once stood.

The only sound now was the rustling of the wind through the trees and the distant chirping of birds. The nightmare was over, and for the first time in what felt like ages, they were truly free.

Chapter 24: Saying Goodbye to Sophie

The sun had fully risen now, casting its warm light across the landscape as the group walked away from the ruins of Grimwood Mansion. The once oppressive and terrifying mansion was gone, dissolved into the morning mist, taking with it the dark history that had haunted it for centuries. It felt surreal, as if the horrors of the previous night had been nothing more than a terrible dream. But the dirt and grime on their clothes and the heaviness in their hearts were proof that it had all been real.

Joe carried the mirror under his arm, the faint shadow of the trapped Shadow Man swirling inside it. His mind was still processing everything they had been through—the battles, the fear, the moments when he thought they might not make it. Yet, there was a lightness to the air now, a sense of freedom that had not been there before. They had survived. They had broken the curse.

Matt walked beside him, still looking pale but stronger with every step. Ann was close by, clutching *The History of Grimwood Manor* to her chest, her eyes scanning the horizon as if trying to fully believe that they were really free. Mandy, her usual upbeat spirit slowly returning, walked a little ahead, kicking at pebbles and occasionally glancing back to make sure everyone was still together.

And then there was Sophie.

Sophie had been quiet since they left the mansion's remains behind, her eyes focused on the rising sun as it bathed the world in golden light. Joe glanced at her, noting the faraway look in her eyes and the way she seemed almost detached from the rest of the group, as if she were walking in a world of her own.

"Sophie," Joe called softly, stepping closer to her. "Are you okay?"

She turned to him slowly, offering a soft smile, but there was something deeply sad in her expression. "I'm... more than okay, Joe," she said quietly. "I'm free."

Ann, overhearing Sophie's words, slowed her pace and looked back, frowning with concern. "What do you mean, Sophie? You've been quiet ever since we left the mansion."

Sophie's smile grew wistful as she glanced at the horizon, the light of the rising sun casting a warm glow on her pale features. "There's something I didn't tell you all," she said, her voice soft, as if she were finally ready to reveal a long-kept secret. "Something I should have told you from the beginning, but I couldn't... not until now."

The group came to a stop, forming a small circle around Sophie as they listened intently. Joe's heart began to pound, sensing that whatever Sophie was about to say would change everything.

"Sophie, what is it?" Mandy asked, her voice filled with concern. "You're scaring me."

Sophie's gaze swept across each of them, her eyes filled with a mixture of sadness and gratitude. "I wasn't just a visitor in the mansion like you," she began, her voice steady but full of emotion. "I've been there for a very long time. Longer than I can even remember."

Ann's eyes widened in shock. "What do you mean? How long?"

Sophie took a deep breath, as if gathering the strength to say what she had kept hidden for so long. "I was one of the first children the Shadow Man trapped in Grimwood Mansion. It was decades ago... maybe even longer. I don't know exactly how much time has passed. I went into that house with my friends, just like you did, thinking it was just an adventure. But we didn't make it out. The Shadow Man... he took us, one by one. I've been trapped there ever since."

The weight of her revelation hit the group like a tidal wave. Joe's stomach churned as he tried to process what Sophie was saying. "You've been trapped... all this time?" he asked, his voice barely above a whisper.

Sophie nodded, her expression filled with sorrow. "Yes. I've watched so many people come and go, trapped just like I was. But none of them ever made it out. I thought I never would either. But then... then you all came, and for the first time, I saw hope. You weren't afraid to stand up to the Shadow Man. You fought back. And because of that, you freed me."

Mandy's eyes filled with tears, and she stepped closer to Sophie, her voice trembling. "You've been stuck there all this time... alone?"

Sophie smiled softly, though her eyes were glassy with unshed tears. "I wasn't always alone. I had my friends for a while, but one by one, the Shadow Man took them. I've spent so many years wandering the mansion, waiting for a way out. But I didn't know if one would ever come."

Ann was staring at Sophie in disbelief, her hands clutching the book tighter. "We never knew. You never said anything."

"I couldn't," Sophie replied, shaking her head gently. "I wasn't sure you'd believe me. And even if you did, I didn't want to burden you with my past. What mattered was finding a way to stop the Shadow Man, to end his curse once and for all. And you did that. You freed me in a way I never thought possible."

Joe felt a lump form in his throat as the truth of Sophie's words sank in. She had been a part of Grimwood Mansion for so long, a lost soul trapped in the shadow of the house's darkness. And now, with the curse broken and the Shadow Man defeated, she could finally be free.

Sophie turned to face the rising sun fully now, her smile bittersweet. "The sun's coming up," she said softly, almost to herself. "I haven't seen the sunrise in... I don't even know how long."

Joe's heart clenched as he noticed something strange. The light of the sun seemed to shine through Sophie more than it did on her. Her figure was becoming hazy, less solid, as if she were fading away into the morning light.

"Sophie?" Ann's voice was filled with panic as she stepped forward, reaching out to her. "What's happening?"

Sophie smiled gently, her eyes filled with peace. "It's time for me to go. Now that the Shadow Man is gone, I'm no longer bound to the mansion. I'm finally free."

Joe's breath caught in his throat. "But... we just found out the truth. We can't lose you now."

"You're not losing me," Sophie said softly, her voice as gentle as the breeze. "You've given me something I never thought I'd have again—freedom. And for that, I'll always be grateful."

As Sophie spoke, her figure became more and more translucent, the edges of her form blending with the light. The group watched in stunned silence, unsure of what to do or say as their friend slowly faded away before their eyes.

Sophie reached into her pocket and pulled out a small, glowing object—a token that shimmered with a soft, ethereal light. She held it out to Joe, her smile warm. "I want you to have this," she said. "A piece of me to remember our time together. You saved me, and I'll never forget that."

Joe, his eyes stinging with unshed tears, reached out and took the glowing token. It was small, round, and warm to the touch, radiating a gentle glow that seemed to pulse with life. "Sophie... thank you."

"Thank you," Sophie whispered, her voice barely audible now. "For everything."

And with that, Sophie's form dissolved completely into the sunlight, leaving nothing but the soft glow of the token in Joe's hand. The group stood in silence, the weight of the moment settling over them like a soft blanket of both sorrow and peace.

Mandy wiped a tear from her cheek, her voice shaky. "She's really gone, isn't she?"

Joe nodded, staring down at the glowing token in his palm. "Yeah. But she's free now. That's what matters."

Ann sniffled softly, her hands trembling as she closed *The History of Grimwood Manor*. "She was with us the whole time, and we didn't even know what she was going through."

"We helped her," Matt said, his voice quiet but steady. "And she helped us. She's at peace now."

Together, the group stood in the warmth of the morning sun, their hearts heavy but filled with a deep sense of gratitude. Sophie had been a part of their journey, and even though she was gone, they knew her spirit would live on in the memories of the night they had all shared.

Chapter 25: The Return Home

The sun had risen high into the sky by the time Joe, Ann, Matt, Mandy, and Sophie made their way back toward town. The morning air was cool and refreshing, a welcome change from the suffocating atmosphere of Grimwood Mansion. Every step they took away from the ruins felt like a release, the tension and fear of the night slowly dissipating with each breath of fresh air. They were tired—bone-tired—but there was a sense of relief and joy in their hearts. They had made it through the night, and now they were finally headed home.

The small dirt path they followed wound its way through the outskirts of town, the early-morning sounds of birds and rustling leaves filling the air. The road was still empty, with most of the town likely still asleep, unaware of the extraordinary adventure the group had just survived.

Joe walked at the front of the group, still carrying the mirror that held the last remnants of the Shadow Man. The faint swirling shadow within had dimmed considerably, a sure sign that his power was completely broken. He glanced back at his friends, smiling to himself. They looked just as exhausted as he felt, but there was a lightness in their steps that hadn't been there before. They had faced their worst fears, fought against an ancient evil, and come out the other side stronger than ever.

Ann walked beside him, clutching *The History of Grimwood Manor* tightly against her chest, as if it were a treasure. Her expression was thoughtful, but there was a small, content smile playing on her lips. She had always been the curious one, eager to learn about the world around her. And now, after everything they'd been through, she had a deeper understanding of what that curiosity could lead to—both good and bad.

"I still can't believe it's over," Ann said softly, breaking the comfortable silence. "The Shadow Man, the mansion... it feels like a dream."

Joe nodded, his voice low and reflective. "Yeah, but it wasn't. We actually did it. We survived."

Matt, who was trailing a little behind them, let out a weak chuckle. "Barely. I don't know about you guys, but I'm looking forward to collapsing in bed and sleeping for about a week."

Mandy grinned, despite the fatigue clearly etched on her face. "You and me both, Matt. I don't think I've ever been this tired in my entire life. But it was worth it, right? We saved each other. We broke the curse."

Sophie, walking quietly next to Mandy, glanced at her with a warm smile. "More than worth it. We did something that most people would have thought impossible."

Joe slowed his pace slightly, letting the group fall into step together. They had gone through so much—individually and as a group—but now, walking down this peaceful road toward home, they were closer than ever before. There was something about surviving an adventure like this that forged bonds in ways nothing else could. They had trusted each other, fought for each other, and stood together against their darkest fears. That kind of bond didn't break.

As the outskirts of the town began to appear in the distance, a strange sense of nostalgia washed over Joe. Halloween decorations still adorned the houses, orange and purple lights flickering in the morning light. A few jack-o'-lanterns sat on porches, their grins now looking a little less ominous after everything they had just faced. The streets were still quiet, but soon enough, the town would wake up and Halloween morning would unfold with its usual charm—innocent fun, costumes, and candy. For everyone else, it would be just another Halloween. But for Joe and his friends, this Halloween had changed everything.

"I never thought Halloween would turn into something like this," Mandy said, looking around at the decorations as they walked. "We were just planning to hang out and eat candy... and then everything changed."

Ann laughed softly, though there was an edge of disbelief in her voice. "Yeah. One minute we're talking about haunted houses, the next minute we're actually trapped in one."

Joe chuckled, shaking his head. "I think this is one Halloween we'll be telling stories about for the rest of our lives."

Matt grinned, though he still looked exhausted. "Can you imagine trying to explain this to anyone? 'Hey, we just spent the night fighting an ancient evil in a haunted mansion, no big deal.' They'd never believe us."

Sophie's smile was wistful, her eyes scanning the horizon as they neared the edge of town. "Maybe they don't have to believe us. This was our adventure. Something we'll carry with us, even if no one else knows what really happened."

Joe nodded in agreement, his heart full as he looked at his friends. "We'll never forget it. No matter what."

The group fell silent for a moment as they crossed into town, the familiar sights of their home making them feel grounded again, like they were finally back where they belonged. The sun was climbing higher now, casting long shadows across the quiet streets. It wouldn't be long before the town would be bustling with people preparing for Halloween festivities. But for the group, the real adventure was already over.

As they approached the park where they had first talked about exploring Grimwood Mansion, Joe slowed his pace and turned to face the others. "Before we go our separate ways... I just want to say thank you."

Ann, Matt, Mandy, and Sophie all looked at him, surprised but smiling.

"For what?" Matt asked, raising an eyebrow.

"For sticking together," Joe said, his voice filled with sincerity. "For having each other's backs, even when things got crazy. I don't think any of us would've made it out of there alone."

Ann nodded, her eyes soft with emotion. "We made it through because we were together. And we're stronger because of it."

Mandy grinned, playfully nudging Joe with her elbow. "What's with the speech? You're getting all emotional on us."

Joe laughed, shaking his head. "I'm serious! This wasn't just some Halloween adventure. It was... something we'll carry with us forever. We all faced our worst fears, and we came out the other side."

Sophie, who had been quiet, stepped forward and smiled softly. "He's right. What we went through will always be a part of us. And no matter where life takes us, we'll always have this bond."

Matt stretched his arms above his head, his grin broad. "Alright, alright. So, we're officially the 'Ghostbusters of Grimwood Mansion.' How about we make a pact?"

Ann tilted her head, intrigued. "A pact?"

Matt nodded, his eyes twinkling mischievously. "Yeah. That we never forget this Halloween and that we always stick together. No matter what happens, we always have each other's backs."

Joe's heart swelled with pride and affection for his friends. It was a simple promise, but it meant the world to him. They had been through something incredible, something that had changed them all. And now, as they stood together on Halloween morning, it felt like the perfect way to honor their journey.

"I'm in," Joe said, raising his hand.

Ann grinned and placed her hand on top of his. "Me too."

Mandy followed suit. "Definitely."

Matt slapped his hand on top of the pile, his grin infectious. "No way I'm backing out now."

Sophie, with a soft, knowing smile, placed her hand on top of theirs. "Forever."

As their hands rested on top of one another, the group made their silent vow, sealing the bond that had been forged in the darkest corners of Grimwood Mansion. They had faced their fears, defeated an ancient evil, and come out the other side stronger and closer than ever. It was a Halloween they would never forget.

With their pact made, the group let out a collective sigh of relief, the weight of the night's events finally lifting from their shoulders. They would return to their homes, their beds, and their normal lives—but they would always carry this adventure in their hearts.

www.ingramcontent.com/pod-product-compliance
Lightning Source LLC
Chambersburg PA
CBHW052045150726
48002CB00002B/753